HOMEWARD BOUND

A SPOUSE'S GUIDE TO REPATRIATION

ROBIN PASCOE

EXPATRIATE PRESS

Vancouver

Expatriate Press Limited
1430 Terrace Avenue
North Vancouver, BC
Canada V7R 1B4
(604) 990-4532
www.expatexpert.com

THIRD PRINTING 2004

ISBN 0-9686760-0-6

Book design by Cardigan Industries
Author photo by Liza Linklater
Printed and bound in Canada

ACKNOWLEDGEMENTS

There are many people to thank for making *Homeward Bound* possible. First and foremost I would like to both thank and acknowledge the tremendous contribution of Joanna Parfitt in bringing *Homeward Bound* to print. An international journalist, author, publisher, and now first class editor, Joanna and I have worked together on *Homeward Bound* since the very beginning when we met at a conference in Paris and decided a book for spouses on the challenges of repatriation was very much needed. Despite the tremendous geographic distance between us (Joanna recently repatriated to the UK while I returned to the west coast of North America) the internet and e-mail have now enabled us to embark on making Expatriate Press a reality. Joanna's tireless promotion, feedback, and editorial skills make *Homeward Bound* as much her book as mine.

I also want to thank Carlanne Herzog for her insightful contributions throughout the book as well as her tremendous foreword, and Kirsten Thogersen for her contributions and for writing an afterword which I believe will leave readers feeling better about themselves. Dave Pollock enjoys world reknown for his work with expatriate children and I was delighted that he found the time to contribute to the families chapter. I am indebted to all the expat spouses world wide who responded to a survey I sent out and who regularly communicate with me through my web site.

Finally, as always, I want to thank Rodney, Lilly and Jamie for putting up with me.

CONTENTS

FOREWORD

by Carlanne Herzog, MA

Over the last twenty years I have experienced four different repatriations and four different overseas assignments and discovered that each one had a different *texture*. I have a masters in psychology and years of personal experience of a mobile lifestyle. For years, I have been professionally involved in the presentation of training courses on transition issues to expatriate communities, with Shell, Schlumberger and StatOil among my many clients. Yet despite all my experience, I have come to learn that I am not immune to the shocks and aftershocks of going home.

The hardest repatriation of all was when we moved back to Texas after an eight year assignment in London. That particular process of grieving lasted more than two years. Since that repatriation, and three subsequent overseas assignments and repatriations, I have had the chance to process everything I have learned and experienced. During this time I have returned to the same country twice (Norway) and am now facing a return to our Texas home for the third time.

I first met Robin Pascoe in Stavanger, Norway, in 1998 when she visited us on a speaking tour. She knows as much about moving and repatriation as anyone who shares her experiences. Only Robin knows, though, how to turn those feelings into words spouses need to read.

When she invited me to write the foreword for this book on going home, I was delighted to have the opportunity to share with you my passion for turning my own experience and research into support and help for others who tread this expatriate road. While I would not want to repeat any of the insights, successes and failures contained in the book, I am pleased, as a 'real life American repatriate' to have the chance to endorse the writings of one 'real life Canadian repatriate', knowing full well that these words will then be edited by a 'real life British repatriate'. Which only goes to show that it doesn't much matter where you have lived or where you were born or to where you return, the journey is much the same. And with that in mind I would like to add my two cents worth of psychologist's insights to this truly inspirational book.

Awareness of each other within the family unit and a willingness to discuss how life is for each person is essential. Repatriation brings with it an external transition period which lasts only the length of the flight home from your foreign assignment to your passport country. Internal transitions, however, move at a far different pace for each family member and require patience and flexibility.

It is perhaps inevitable that throughout the shifting sands and emotions of an international move, or a repatriation, that it is the mother who has to be the stabilising influence of life at home. It is the mother who is required repeatedly to put her own wishes and needs to one side. The life lived by the international expatriate spouse is one of constant reassessment and new goal setting. Each family member has his or her own agenda.

Every move requires what I call 'a suitcase of skills', and it is usually up to the mother, again, to make sure they have all been packed. A sense of humour is vital of course, but try not to forget to be clear about the motivation for the move and challenges you are likely to face. Low goal and task orientation should be packed along with realistic expectations and an ability to fail.

Making a move as a family puts a lot of pressure on that family to communicate effectively. Each family member has his or her own needs, which, if left unmet, can lead to insecurity and unhappiness. Often the immediate family unit is the only constant or 'thread of continuity' that can be expected to run from country to country and then home again.

But, just as it is impossible to deny the importance and relevance of the happiness of family members both in and out of work, neither can we forget the value of making friends and maintaining the interests that make up our personality.

When we return home we have been altered by our time overseas. Issues that never affected us before, such as materialism, we may now find impossible to come to terms with. Reverse culture shock in its many manifestations, can deal a harsher blow than the culture shock we had expected abroad. Now the pace of life seems to have altered, our diaries are mysteriously empty, and the paradigms we used to make up our view of a normal world all seem to have shifted. If you return from a culture that had a flexible attitude to time keeping, but a strong sense of family, you may find yourself questioning your own beliefs on repatriation.

You changed while you were abroad. The people you left behind will have moved on too. It's as if, as

Robin so accurately describes, 'you have your contact lenses in the wrong eyes.' Everything is just about the same and totally different at the same time.

While some change can energise and motivate us, when we find too many values in our home country conflict with those we've forged in foreign assignments, we feel immobilised with so much change.

There can be a sense of real loss for some family members. Symbols, such as the flag of a foreign country, are no longer seen. We are perhaps assailed by the different attitudes towards dress in our home country. Although we are perhaps fortunate enough to relocate closer to our own kin, those friends who became like family to us in our foreign country setting are sorely missed. We may find ourselves drawn to an ethnic restaurant reminiscent of the country we've left behind. We can feel ambivalent about everything.

Adapting to a foreign country wasn't easy either, was it? As always, it goes back to recognising the stages of transition you have to go through. The three stages of transition involve endings, a wilderness period which may be protracted, and new beginnings. Understanding where you are in this process might not lift your blue mood but you can feel safe in the knowledge that you will survive. Transitions are external and internal. Externally, your life is turned upside down – and very quickly too when you consider how long the flight back to your passport country actually took. Internally, each family member must progress mentally and emotionally to once again feel that they fit into their home country.

Moving is not just a physical activity. It requires an overabundance of mental and emotional energy. Forcing yourself to have all the pieces of your life in place as soon as possible may spell disaster.

While you are adjusting, keep Robin's book handy. Dip into it as you experience every stage of return culture shock, safe in the knowledge that you are not alone.

Carlanne Herzog · 2000

INTRODUCTION

On a clear and crisp summer morning, the perfect Canadian weather I used to daydream about when we lived in sweltering Asian capitals, I was invited to tell my intercultural story to a group of cross-cultural trainers gathered in Vancouver at the University of British Columbia. It was almost two years to the day since our re-entry to a new life on the west coast of Canada.

Arriving at the campus early, I parked myself on an outdoor bench with a Starbucks latte, and gazed out at the postcard scenery which tourists flock to my country to see. I sat alone, overwhelmed and intimidated by the sheer size of the magnificent coastal mountains surrounding me. I sensed my solitary view of that remarkable vista was a metaphor for how I felt about leaving expatriate life. The vastness of the landscape represented the wide spectrum of experience I had gained by living abroad. My loneliness was the price to be paid for deciding to stay put and relinquishing responsibility for constant packing and farewells.

But later, when the time came to stand before my audience, serious mountain metaphors seemed best kept to myself. I decided to begin my remarks simply. "My story is about coming home."

"It's a happy/sad/happy/sad/happy/sad/happy/sad story depending on the time of day, the way my hair looks, if I have been able to make eye contact with even one stranger, whether it has stopped raining long enough for me to see the sun, or if my husband is in or out of town, in which case I will blame him for all of the above."

So much for any great philosophical insights. I'm really just a stand up comic at heart.

That day happened to be a happy one for I was surrounded by people who knew that re-entry had nothing to do with astronauts and the earth's gravitational force. I could speak in the shorthand language of those who have lived or worked abroad, using expressions I had deliberately expunged from my conversation with new neighbours and friends because, to them, I might as well have been speaking in tongues.

Trusting my audience to understand my feelings of reverse culture shock, I could be honest about the challenges posed by my re-entry. I felt safe confessing that in the two years leading up to that particular day (two years that flew by so fast I could hardly believe that in the same space of time in the past, I would have packed up my family, settled them into yet another foreign land, lived the full and rich life of an expatriate, packed up again and moved on) there had been too many dark and depressing days where I could barely pull myself together. Storm clouds had gathered over my new home on a regular basis during those years, and not all of them could be blamed on the rainy Vancouver weather or that convenient whipping boy, my husband. Some of them linger still.

Re-entry. Repatriation. Resettlement. Returning home. These are just some of the words commonly used to refer to the closing chapter in an expatriate's overseas life. They are all good, solid, meaningful words. But they stop short of one very critical other 'r' word: *Reality*. Reality is the very real world of home, wherever that may be in the world, and a far cry from what many returnees have described as the fairy tale existence their lives used to be.

Moving home after living abroad for months or years can be one of life's sweetest pleasures, especially if the move has been voluntary and well-planned. The moment the wheels of your plane touch down on your native soil is one to be savoured. You happily listen to instructions being barked out over the loudspeaker in a familiar language and enter into an airport which, even if caught up in rush hour madness, is nonetheless culturally familiar. It doesn't matter if there are long lineups at immigration control, no luggage trolleys in sight, or a taxi to get you out of there. The stuff that made you crazy in foreign airports now just rolls off your back. You want to tell everyone within hearing distance how glad you are to be home. You drive your kids nuts rhapsodising over this return home and they roll their eyes at you. But you don't care. You are home! Let the new life begin!

Not so fast.

Those three short words should become a mantra for repatriated partners. Absolutely nothing will be fast about the re-entry exercise. This is the first and most important reality check you need to make. A new life will not happen overnight, no matter how hard you will desperately wish that were the case. Patience has never been one of my own virtues, but I wish someone had told me how critical it would be if I wanted to keep my life from derailing emotionally.

There have been numerous studies by management consulting firms around the world that indicate the re-entry experience for the working partner is not as good as it should be. As many as 40% of returning employees quit within two years depending on whose figures you are reading. But in these pages, I won't be spouting numbers, nor will I devote much attention to the working partner, except for the ways that person's adjustment may impact on the non-working partner. Those readers familiar with my other two books on expatriate adjustment *A Wife's Guide* and *A Parent's Guide* know where my loyalties in this exercise lie. I will once again be focusing my attention on the experience of the partner, and especially the female partner, who doesn't immediately go off to headquarters or a new job.

Like the move abroad, the move home relies on a solid and stable person to act as the emotional touchstone in order to help everyone else in the family through the adjustment period. That someone is typically the spouse and, as usual, our needs come last on the list, too often because we put them there ourselves.

The re-entry process and the adjustments the partner need to make to being home are a lot tougher than they would seem. Hampering the process is a misguided belief by many that they will have absolutely no adjustments to make in coming home. It's home isn't it? This is what most people tell themselves, and then do nothing to prepare themselves for the re-entry shocks which lie ahead, like building a life all over again. Worse still, once home, they ignore the ups and downs and general malaise that can settle in after a few months until one day it just hits them between the eyes that they are desperately unhappy when they clearly shouldn't be, but can't explain why.

Like culture shock, re-entry shock is fortunately not a terminal disease. It has a cycle of its own and mercifully, it ends. It just doesn't end overnight, and I believe every returning partner should know about it well in advance if only for the reassurance that you are not alone in experiencing it.

In complete contrast to your arrival abroad, where someone might have picked you up at the airport and whisked you away to a home often pre-selected, already furnished, and a fridge filled with a welcome goodie pack, there is no welcome wagon when you come home. The working partner may even be at the office or conveniently on a road trip the day the moving boxes arrive. There are no community services centers or expatriate counsellors around to help you either. Looking for a new house? The prices may trigger your re-entry shock. Looking for work? For some, it can be more challenging to find employment at home than abroad. Thinking about having another baby? Facing a mid-life crisis? Menopause? We'll get to all of these subjects later. For now, it's important to know that these challenges do exist, but the same positive attitude that helped you live the full, rich life of an expatriate will help you get over these hurdles too.

Many people asked me to write this book when I first came home, but I knew I couldn't possibly do it then. I had to experience my own re-entry shock first. I had to make a lot of the mistakes that I can now hopefully help others avoid or at least minimise.

Some of the same reasons which motivated my earlier books, especially my expat wife *manifesto* as my husband refers to it, apply again. No one told me any-

thing about what to expect. I had no support from
others in the same boat. I moped around, my moods
swinging up and down, allowing those dark clouds
to ruin sunny days because I didn't know some of my
reactions to coming home were perfectly natural.

There are many reasons why expatriates choose to
move home and I will try to cover most of them in
these pages. What precipitated our own move home?
After fifteen years in the Canadian foreign service
which finished up in Seoul, my husband and I decided
to change our lives, that is, my husband's job, which
in addition to South Korea, had taken us to Bangkok,
Taipei, and Beijing. We moved to Vancouver in beautiful British Columbia. With our two young children
packed off to summer camps in central Canada, we
flew into our new city on a glorious summer evening.
Even arriving at a house full of storage boxes half
opened couldn't dampen my pleasure. I was home!

Well, sort of. We had never lived in Vancouver before. We knew very few people and none who had
ever lived abroad and could understand what we
were going through. My children were certainly not
going to meet other mobile children in our suburb
of North Vancouver where my son Jamie, upon entering grade four at the time, so eloquently pointed
out that his classmates had not only been playing
together since kindergarten but since they were in
diapers! My husband Rodney's new job carried so
many travel commitments we would never have contemplated possible. In fact, he was gone on a long
working trip within weeks of our arrival – but not
before he advised me to get my résumé in order and
start making a few phone calls. Was he out of his
mind? It was obviously going to be the shortest honeymoon period on record.

Even though I had arrived in a picture-perfect heaven, with a storybook village ten minutes by foot away and mountains and a rain forest in my back yard, I gradually began to feel the emotional weight of those moving boxes. Despite re-entering on two other occasions in another part of Canada where I could at least find support from other foreign service wives like me, I was spiralling into re-entry shock but didn't recognise the signs. I figured I was tired, lethargic, depressed and totally unmotivated – a person completely unfamiliar to me – because I had made five international moves over eight summers. Only a robot wouldn't be exhausted. I also wasn't aware yet how muddled and confused ordinary life passages can become with re-entry shock.

It also took me a while to realise that most people simply don't have or make time for new friends. I constantly ask those I am meeting for the first time: when was the last time you made a new friend? I am not surprised when they say they can't remember. Throw into this mix the social impact of technology, the so-called ease of computers and e-mail which has complicated and isolated people's lives, as well as all the political and economic changes to your home country, and there is a lot to handle besides unpacking a few boxes.

I didn't give much structured thought to any of my feelings until I was invited to The Hague to speak to Royal Dutch/Shell partners at their first Outpost Global Conference. Much to my delight, Shell partners continue to get a lot out of my earlier books for expatriate spouses and parents. Speaking in the morning to Shell's in-country counsellors who run their OUTPOST network, I was then asked if I would speak again in the afternoon to Shell partners who had reentered and were not going off abroad again. Merely as an aside to my prepared talk, I told this repatriated group how tired and worn out I felt and how much I suffered from what I had loftily decided to call *cumulative culture shock fatigue* from making too many moves. If I wasn't so tired, I joked, I would write a book about it. The audience immediately latched onto that comment. "Please write about that," they said.

I think you will recognise your own story in my narrative, or certainly good chunks of it. At the very least, please read these pages and have a laugh or a good therapeutic cry where appropriate. Allow some of your own dark clouds to disappear to make room for the sun that, honestly, will come out tomorrow.

ONE

SO YOU HAVE DECIDED TO MOVE HOME

THINGS TO CONTEMPLATE BEFORE YOU LEAVE
THE POST

"At the time, I thought returning home to the USA would resolve all our problems."
> – a 37-year-old American woman on why she and
> her husband decided to return home.

Three months before moving home to Canada from Seoul, a move supposed to be our last relocation, a final off-the-wall adventure seemed called for and preferably by myself. Since the locale needed to be memorable, I chose an Indian *ashram* nestled in a lost horizon in the Himalayas populated oddly enough by fellow Canadians, including an older male cousin from Nova Scotia who moved there in the 1970s. Running away to a club meditation which offered both long lost family and an enlightened guru seemed the perfect activity for a middle-aged woman desperate to think about anything but moving boxes. Contemplating the universe seemed much easier than figuring out what was left to buy in Asia.

In the weeks leading up to the trip, full scale anxiety attacks were a regular feature of my sleepless nights. I redirected onto my India escapade my rising panic about the impact of the coming repatriation, producing angst of the most superficial variety. For instance, I fretted for weeks over the *ashram* wardrobe

I needed to take to India as dictated over the phone by my cousin. Only long sleeved shirts and long skirts were acceptable, he had shouted down the static-filled lines from Kullu in the Indian province of Himal Pradesh, and certainly nothing provocative (as if such articles of clothing existed in my closet).

Ironically, my quest for the meaning of my new life would begin in the street boutiques of the Iaetewon district of Seoul, combing the endless piles of flawed designer clothing (with long sleeves) in underground shopping markets. Catching sight of myself in the cracked mirror of a so-called dressing room (a sheet pulled around a space the size of a bucket) I would try not to laugh out loud at the fortysomething flower child with a slightly desperate look in her eyes peering back at me.

A wonderful new job awaited my husband in Vancouver. Yet another reinvention lay ahead for me. Of course, my future could only begin after settling in and organising our two children, Lilly and Jamie, respectively 13 and 9 at the time. My husband kindly offered me an air ticket to make a house hunting trip from Seoul to Vancouver. Aware of the difficult months ahead, it seemed a much better proposition to take an adventure holiday in the opposite direction. I bravely told my partner that he could go and buy a house alone. I would take my chances and was prepared to live with whatever bathrooms came with the new house. My girlfriends thought my decision to let my husband buy a house without me infinitely more daring than travelling solo to India in hippie garb with only a reasonable facsimile of a knapsack on my back.

Feeling Life Will End Upon Re-entry

This was more than just a case of trying to pass personal muster. True, who wouldn't want to prove they still possessed the nerve and independence to pull off what everyone thinks is a crackpot trip? But I was trapped in a dangerous pre-re-entry mindset endemic to the going home exercise.

I believed the interesting part of my life would abruptly end the minute I became a repatriate instead of expatriate.

The *ashram*, which is equal parts Meditation University, intellectual spa, and nifty place to go, represented more than just a wild and crazy 'last hurrah.' I needed help in understanding what lay ahead. A swami, sitting on a scenic mountain top with a long white beard, a hearty laugh, and flowing bright robes seemed a reasonable, if slightly unconventional, coach. At least I could contemplate my future with a man who wouldn't be as sick of discussing the subject as much my own man clearly was getting to be.

During my visit, I kept a diary I cheekily entitled *Desperately Seeking Enlightenment and Cheap Rugs*. (When I would mention that title to others, the automatic question was: cheap drugs? No, I would have to say on many occasions, rugs!) But my diary scribblings were so honest and candid I only claim now I must have been high: on Himalayan air. Since my cousin had enjoyed it so much (he made me read it out loud in the evenings to members of his community, much to my dismay) I later mailed it to him as a gift. Apparently, my observations validated many of the *ashram's* members choice to live in India, so my cousin decided to make several hundred copies so that *complete strangers* living or travelling in the

Himalayas could share my deepest, most personal thoughts and send home copies to *their* friends and families. Years later, I have almost but not quite forgiven him. (At the time of writing, he was still handing out copies).

My Indian diary is a revealing document of my expectations of a new post-expatriate life. Consider this entry in which I contemplated my new home office: "I can't wait to design my new work space in Vancouver," I wrote at 5:30 one morning when coffee and the stress of being surrounded by people who do nothing but think deep thoughts all day combined to shift my brain into overdrive. "I want the space to be in the fashion of the beautiful spaces I have seen here in Kullu. I want my work area to provide me with the calm and serenity I feel here, with cushions down on the floor and everything close to the ground – the earth – the source of life on earth. I don't think I have to ask to do this either. I just can. I feel I can do anything now."

Writing at high altitudes from an *ashram* in a place called the Valley of the Gods obviously skewers reality heavily on the side of optimism. Positive thinking isn't necessarily a bad thing, of course, but only if you remember that you do have to come down from the mountain one day. In the new house I had never seen because I had sent my husband off to buy it, there would actually be no office space whatsoever for me, just a corner of a family room where the walls would have to spring from my own vivid imagination until we could afford drywall.

The swami – who was lovely by the way and doesn't deserve my irreverence – explained patiently to me that if I really wanted to understand the change that lay ahead for me, I should begin by understanding the notion of *unchange*. That's really not as cosmic as it may sound. This learned man was trying to drive home the point to me that while my physical environment may change (compare Seoul to Vancouver and you get my drift), the qualities that make me 'me' would remain the same. He was advising me to exercise patience and allow my transformation the time it needed to take place. He also told me to stay away from negative people because they would only hinder my happiness. All good, positive advice which I quickly ignored as soon as I survived the flight back from Kullu to New Delhi in an airplane Stephen Spielberg surely used as a prop in his Indiana Jones series. (Thinking positively, though, the hair-raising flight did obliterate my fear of flying. I still chant the swami's *mantra* whenever I take off and discovered I am much calmer and less hung over than the days I used my former 'martini' *mantra*.)

Fear of flying forgotten after my spiritual adventure, I also conveniently blotted out of my mind that in Vancouver (where people move *to* not *from*), I would have neither support nor empathy from gurus or at the very least, like-minded repatriates who could share their experiences of change, and of settling down after too many years on the move.

I would also have neither re-entry training nor a counsellor to guide me. I would barely have my partner around because of his excessive travel commitments. And with my extended family living on the other side of Canada, my support system would be severely limited. I feared my new life would get bogged down admiring all that gorgeous British Columbia scenery. That would cover about five minutes of my day. I had to figure out how I would spend the rest of my day and I would have to do it for the most part, alone.

It wasn't enough for me to read about all the adjustments my husband (that is, the employee) would have
to make. I felt enough was written and documented
about re-entry shock in the corporate world with only
snippets of advice to those of us who trail behind,
packing and unpacking that employee and his children's lives. It seemed that most companies choose to
simply brainwash their employees into believing there
will be no problems moving home so that in turn, the
employee can spout that inane (and totally incorrect)
message to a wife who is lying comatose on her bed
from exhaustion, depression or both.

If you are about to depart for home, or thinking
about it, or looking back on it now and don't have an
Indian guru handy for consultation, what follows are
answers to questions that even my swami couldn't
contemplate.

Why Do Expats Choose to Become Repats?

To truly understand where the re-entry process springs
from, it's important to identify the factors which
cause families to choose to move home, temporarily
or forever. Our own decision to put aside moving
boxes for good was motivated by many factors, some
of which are not at all uncommon beginning with:

Age, Stage, and Health of Children or Parents

Many expats choose to come home when their children, often their eldest, reach high school age. Moving around with children becomes increasingly difficult during the teenage years. It seems to defy a law
of nature to uproot a teenager from their friends and
activities in high school. Not only is it important to
allow a child to stay put during those years, it could
be that like we did, you would like your children

to know about the country stamped on the cover of their own passport. It may also be that you have placed your child in a boarding school and have grown weary of the constant back and forth travelling required to nurture from abroad.

Early childhood in four Asian postings provided our own children with a foundation for learning for which I will always be grateful. The absence of commercial television in their early years was by itself worth all the moving around for its positive influence on them.

As many parents may finally decide, however, there are some tradeoffs that can become too much to make. Childhood comes around only once, and I personally didn't want the balance of my young children's lives hanging too much on the side of academics and desperately long rides on school buses to international schools with little free time to goof off, be able to ride bikes, and get around town on their own. Likewise, while it is certainly wonderful and educational to appreciate other cultures, what about knowing their own?

Other parents contemplating re-entry don't have the luxury of thinking about childhood activities. These are the parents of children with health issues, like breathing problems in polluted capitals, children with learning disabilities not handled adequately by the international school system, or tragically worse, illnesses too awful to contemplate. Those parents will also reach a point where going home becomes the only viable option for the sake of their children.

For still others, it could be a parent's poor health and the unavailability of a sibling to look after that parent. Linda, a Canadian diplomatic acquaintance of mine, came home to look after both her own ageing mother as well as her husband's. She offered words I'm sure will resonate with others: "She really needed me," she told me, referring to her own mother and their decision to effectively retire early. "She needed the hands-on care and consideration that you can only give on the spot."

Professional Mid-life Crisis

Beginning anywhere from the mid 30's to mid 40's, the professional mid-life crisis looms out there like a virus that has to be lived through. When it is primarily your partner's issue and not your own, you may feel helpless standing by watching him struggle over what to do about it, if anything.

He may be bored in his job, see no opportunity for advancement, or just be thinking that he is still young enough to begin something new if he could just figure out what that 'something' might be. Worse still, you may hit a devastating life stage where friends the same age as you are falling ill with terminal diseases. *Life is too short and precious.* That becomes an infinitely more serious refrain in your mind than wondering about exotic travel opportunities or complaining about traffic. It makes the idea of change before it is too late an attractive option.

The thought of leaving a structure and striking out on his own may both terrify and excite your partner. If he is asking himself "is this all there is?" he might need a friendly, supportive push to help him find meaningful post-expatriate employment.

Having worked in our government's foreign service for fifteen years, the idea of leaving a structure initially bewildered my own partner as much as terrified him, and not because he didn't have the right stuff for another job. He just didn't know how to make the quantum leap from the security of a government position to the uncertainty and potential rejection of the working world at large. I helped him through the process of assessing his skills, his strengths and weaknesses, and making suggestions as to who best might want to utilise them.

Wife Wants a Career Before It's Too Late to Try

I should know better than to even use that dreaded word *career*. Readers familiar with *A Wife's Guide* will know that I constantly advise women not to get hung up on that word and look at the career issue in the context of the mobile expatriate life. Having said that, I will also remind readers that I never said that I take my own advice.

Like men reaching their professional mid-life crisis, women aren't exempt from the condition either. I will reserve comment until Chapter Five which is devoted to career and life issues. Many spouses give up careers to follow partners abroad. Some harbour anger and resentment over never having had a clean shot at any satisfying work. Those spouses one day may finally throw up their arms and say: "Right! It's my turn now. But we need to stay put somewhere in order for me to even try."

Downsizing and Restructuring

A more serious factor forcing expatriates home has been major shifts in the overseas workplace. Not only are expatriate managers being replaced with locals, a process that began long before some economies started to get into trouble, but corporate downsizing and restructuring has turfed many an expat executive out of an overseas job. Worsening matters further have been tumbling global economies and the drop in prices for many commodities.

When the re-entry decision comes up fast, without warning as it has for many in recent years, it makes the idea of understanding re-entry and all its ramifications even more critical because it's not something which has been thought through or planned properly. On top of that may be a terrible layer of insecurity and feelings of worthlessness on the part of the working partner who suddenly finds himself out of a job. Worse, when he comes home, he may literally have nothing to do all day, especially if he goes into a forced retirement. The anger and resentment cycle can shift over to his side. A good Australian friend who prefers to remain anonymous confirms this happened to her. While she went out and tried to get her life going again once home in Sydney, she felt her husband was annoyed by her activity and in her words, 'grunted' at her in the early days of their return, trouncing her self-esteem and de-motivating her when she was already struggling to find her energy again.

Retirement or Worse, Ill Health, Divorce or Death

Retirement is usually mapped out well in advance but even the best laid plans can go awry. Likewise, just because you have planned your re-entry doesn't mean there still won't be shocks, like the end of a marriage. Husbands leave wives all the time, but when they do it during an overseas assignment as has happened for many women, going home with the experience of a global life is less triumphant and more demoralising. An American woman married almost twenty years (again, she prefers anonymity) wrote to tell me that her own ex-husband waited until they returned home to inform her he was leaving her. He quickly returned to where they had just left to be with a new partner propelling her, she writes, "into a mid-life crisis full of self-doubt, depression, stress and health problems." Not exactly the welcome home anyone would want.

Worse to contemplate, is the sudden death of a partner. I have met expatriate widows who never expected after living abroad for twenty or thirty years to suddenly lose their partner overseas. If re-entry is a shock to the system (and Chapter Two will detail some of those shocks), can there be anything more stressful than the sudden death of the spouse? Under those circumstances, re-entry has challenges no one can ever prepare you for.

Inge, a Canadian friend of mine, lost her husband to cancer when they were living in China. She has blocked out many of her memories of such a horrible time, but did offer some important tips for coping which I think are worth passing along here. Inge's advice applies to women who suddenly find themselves alone, whether through death or divorce:

Try to be in a secure community. It's important to have family and friends around you.

There is usually a great deal to do in the first weeks. If you can find someone who is reliable and who you trust to act as your 'right hand' it is enormously helpful.

The people who will be most useful and helpful to you at this time are your doctor, a minister or a rabbi if you are religious, your lawyer and your accountant. A good relationship with your banker is also helpful.

Seek counselling if you feel you need it. Don't feel badly if you need sleeping pills or anti-depressants to help you through this initial period.

Often, six months after the death (or divorce) is an unexpectedly difficult time. The shock is wearing off and the reality begins to sink in.

Don't attempt to do too much too soon. Certainly don't make any major new decisions during the first year after the death (or divorce) unless absolutely necessary.

THEMES FOR REALISTIC RE-ENTRY DISCUSSIONS

Allow me to raise some serious talking points which may prove helpful in having a realistic discussion with your partner about the move home. You need to raise these issues while you are still living overseas before any decision is taken. Some of these questions are certainly based on my own experience and those of others, and might help keep at least some of your expectations for a smooth emotional adjustment rooted firmly on the ground. So begin with:

Is Moving Home a Joint Decision?

When one partner is against the idea of re-entry, or worse, isn't consulted beforehand and just informed of an imminent repatriation, the resulting emotional fallout can be devastating. This certainly was the case for Mary, a Canadian friend of mine now living in The Netherlands after twenty years of expatriate life. She had never contemplated living in Holland (the country of her husband's birth), and was informed about the move over the phone from a third country where her husband was working on a short term assignment. She was just told to pack up everything and be ready to move two months later.

"The shock, anger and resentment were indescribable," she told me. Far from being a joint decision, she felt it was autocratic and almost dealt a near fatal blow to her relationship with her husband. Five years after the move, she feels back on track but her advice to others I believe is worth passing along. "If we had been able to reach the decision to relocate together", she says, "countless instances of needless pain and fury could have been avoided."

Are You Thinking of Moving to a Place Where You Have a Ready-made Community or Will You Need to Re-build One?

It would seem that it is the norm for people to return 'home' and have some new element to deal with: either a new city altogether, or a new house in an old home base, or building a new network of friends and contacts. For some, repatriation isn't exactly a true expression as they are moving to their partner's home culture. Whatever the new twist in your tale, it's a good idea to have a few ideas of what to expect before the shock of that newness, whatever it may be, is thrust upon you and your partner.

Of all the adjustments I have had to make as a returning expat wife, the toughest has been moving to a Canadian city that I had never lived in before. I had moved around Canada quite a bit before I was married, but never lived on the west coast where I have no history or family, no feelings of connection or community. I would never say that Vancouver is the worst city I have ever lived in for if this is hell, it's certainly a beautiful hell.

But it's tough to move to a city and into neighbourhoods where people have lived all their lives. There are few people who can remotely picture the life you have led, creating a huge *experience gap* especially lacking in shared history. This is sort of like those Home Leave conversations which every expat dreads because no one wants to hear your stories. Going home, there will also be the same blank stares and quick changes of subjects when overseas life comes up. Only in this case, you don't return at the end of six weeks to people who understand what you are talking about.

Factor in this nugget of insight I quickly figured out and put into words for myself before I started to take rejection from new people so personally: Overseas, it is the norm to speak to people you don't know. At home, people tend to limit themselves to people they do know. For the expat spouse, who needs only to catch the eye in a grocery store abroad of another spouse who looks to be in the same boat, (that's how I met so many of my friends) and a lengthy conversation usually begins, it can be disconcerting to discover you can't even make eye contact at home.

Depending on your age and stage at the time of re-entry, it's easy to forget that you used to make friends when your children were younger while waiting with other parents at the pre-school, organised play groups, or elementary school plays. There was something about that mutual exhaustion which helped build great friendships that seemed to endure. Everyone you met had no time other than that devoted to their children, so your time lines crossed and you were literally thrown together.

This may not be the case when your children get older and begin having lives of their own. You merely drop them off somewhere without long detailed conversations or interaction with another parent. It's hard to make a connection unless it was made ten years earlier in pre-school. For the returning spouse who spent those years on the move, your closest friends are only available for regular e-mail chats, not for coffee, and that can make you feel very lonely at first.

Carlanne Herzog, a psychologist who has worked extensively with expatriate families, reminds us that patterns of friendships do vary.

"You may have found locals friendly and outgoing in Venezuela or Texas but quite reticent in Northern Europe. It is worth noting that the term 'friend' is defined differently by individuals and cultures. While some would call an 'acquaintance' a 'friend' others would use the word 'friend' only to describe someone who shared their life goals and values," she says.

Don't expect to much of yourself. Remember that eventually you *will* make new friends, but it takes time.

Will Your Partner Have a New Job Right Away? If So, Will He Travel?

This is like a good news/bad news joke. I'll begin with the good: your partner scores a great new job outside of his company (or even within) and is happy, challenged, stimulated and then comes the bad news: he is absolutely never home! You don't know whether to laugh or cry. You are pleased that something has worked out so well for him personally (and hence the family) but you suddenly realise that the terrific new job will take him away from home several weeks every month. This can happen easily to men who move outside their old jobs, because after all, what is their expertise? International work! And where does that occur? In the international marketplace which is definitely not in your new neighbourhood.

A major headache of the adjustment period of my own family was getting used to the constant travel imposed by my husband's new job. I ended up blaming everything difficult about our new lives on his travel schedule which was obviously grossly unfair of me. But in the throes of my re-entry shock, I simply could not get past the idea that we had made a move supposedly to allow me to begin a 'career' and how exactly could I do that when our children needed a parent to help them settle in? I had become, essentially, a single parent without dating privileges. (I certainly told him this often enough.)

It can be bad news to have a partner without a job who returns to headquarters to stare at files all day in an empty office (if he's lucky). Or a partner who has an unsuitable job that doesn't utilise all the skills and experience he gained abroad. That happened to the husband of Sue, a UK repat spouse whose husband's company brought him home after nine years away only to put him in a position which was definitely not commensurate with his experience and knowledge. Sue reported to me that her husband's situation made her feel "pretty helpless as I was trying to settle everybody in and had not made the contacts to enable me to work and make money." She definitely advises that the working partner spend time before coming home sorting out with the company what job he will do next as one way of avoiding what her husband went through.

Neither scenario makes it easy for the spouse to get on with life. It can take some time to work through these challenges and often will require the help of a professional counsellor. Don't be afraid to engage one.

Will Your Children Still Require a Lot of Attention and Support?

Never assume that just because you are moving to a nice, safe area where your child can walk to school that everything will be rosy. Of course, it's wonderful to watch as your children begin to thrive in their own culture and enjoy the physical freedom that might have been denied them at the post.

But like moving overseas, it will take a lot of time and energy to settle your children, especially in another city that is new to them. Don't forget to factor their adjustment period into your own expectations and how much of it will rest on your shoulders. You may even be considering having another child now that you are home again. With these challenges on the horizon, be realistic when assessing the time frame for your resettlement.

Are Your Finances in Shape? Can You Afford to Move and Still Live as You Want?

Depending on where you decide to move, there may be a few lifestyle changes in store for you and your partner, some of them good, and some of them challenging. A lot of them will center around money. Having selected a place to move to, can you afford it? Will you be able to afford the luxuries you took for granted abroad since they were paid for as part of your package? These questions take us back to the subject of unrealistic expectations about what home will be like.

We knew, for instance, moving to Vancouver was going to be an expensive proposition. Real estate prices were outrageous, never mind everything else we might have decided the family had to have now that we were back. (Skiing, for instance, is not a cheap sport but with the world's best just down the road at Whistler, was there any question it wouldn't become a necessity from our over-privileged viewpoint rather than a luxury?)

Let me say this straight: overseas we often live very pampered lives. Re-entry into the real world can be 'flying money' time. So much goes out the window when you first get home and settle in that suddenly, what you figured was an appropriate 'start up' cost based on your savings just seems like lunch money. Furthermore, life in many Western countries is predicated on two incomes, not one with lots of overseas benefits. That second income will take a little while to secure.

With hindsight, I certainly would have stayed away from bank machines to let less money fly away. I would have also insisted more vehemently that if my husband's employer was so keen on having him, he had better think about doing more for me, his spouse.

What About Telling The Children?

I have written in *A Parent's Guide* and will continue to stress that children of a certain age absolutely must be brought into discussions which involve a family move. At the same time, I have always added my own caveat: just because you are asking them for their input doesn't mean that you aren't going to ultimately move in the end. Your opinion obviously is the most important, but children should never be made to feel that they weren't consulted and that a move, whether home or abroad, is a done deal before they can even get an opinion out of their mouths.

You moved abroad as a family. You move home as a family. Everyone, including the children, must have their say about it in order that they become a stakeholder, that is, someone whose needs count. Children respond immediately and viscerally to suggestions of change (the 'you're ruining my life!' response springs from that) but equally get over things a lot quicker than adults. Remember, though, that if you say that you are going home for the children's sake, it's a good idea to find out if they happen to agree.

When children are not told the entire truth, they will believe what they will. If you don't tell them, they will make assumptions that may be so far off base that it will take a lot of persuasion to bring them back to reality. They often tend to think the worst. Like parents everywhere, you want your children to enjoy that sense of security and safety which parents work hard to provide while they are still under your roof and your care. They will not feel safe if they feel information is being withheld and something may be going on that seems 'scary' but they don't know why. The change brought about by moving home is frightening enough for some children (they immediately think of saying goodbye to friends and a new strange school they can't picture looms in their imaginations) so don't make it worse. Besides, as a family you now have plans to make for how you are going to handle the family's pre-departure farewells.

More Questions Later

There are other issues that need to be raised, like job skills, life stage and so on which will be raised in the coming chapters. For now, while sitting abroad, begin your discussion with these. And be sure to keep the volume down on these discussions. Like moving abroad, your children must feel moving home is a united decision and everything is just fine, thanks, between mom and dad.

The Importance of Saying Goodbye

When expat families leave a post, a lot of fuss is typically made, despite the fact that people leave all the time. There are special parties for adults, luncheons for women, and if the international school is a good one, closing ceremonies that not only hand out awards but also make a point of saying farewell to those students leaving. Seoul Foreign School, our last international school experience, handles the closing beautifully with a ceremony that provides a sense of closure not only to the school year, but for those departing children's experience in Korea.

If you live in places where these events don't naturally occur, organise them yourselves, especially for your children, and most especially if you are bringing to an end the overseas chapter of their lives. I don't suggest you send children off by themselves to an *ashram* in India as I went in order to bolster my sense of independence, but the idea of setting up some interesting trip or adventure or anything (a party works too) that they will remember forever is worth the time and effort. Drive around and re-visit places where happy events took place so that everyone can say goodbye to not only people, but 'place' as well. Make sure children resolve outstanding disputes with their friends so they don't think they can spend the rest of their lives resolving issues by just leaving. Make special remembrance books with pictures or postcards. This applies to both children and adults because they will serve as physical reminders of your time abroad that are not just caught in memory and like a student high school year book, can be poured over in later years. Definitely make a list of e-mail addresses.

Three Important Phases to Understand

Making a point of saying goodbye to everyone, everything, indeed, every place that was part of your overseas life (even the freedom to do exotic trips) is an important part of the three-step re-entry process which begins with:

1. *Closure*

There's nothing mysterious about the concept of closure but you would be surprised how many people think it's unnecessary or merely applies only to goodbye parties. Closure is much more profound an emotional experience than gaining five pounds at your own farewell dinner parties. It's allowing your mind to move freely on to the next chapter in your life without constantly feeling the urge to flip back to refer to earlier pages. That's not to say that the book is never re-opened with memories or emotions or conversational anecdotes (even when the person listening gives you a blank stare). Nor does it mean that earlier parts of your life won't impact positively on the next part. Learning to value your overseas experience is a subject handled in Chapter Five.

When you set up the means which provide closure to an experience, you are allowing yourself the capacity to allow yourself to grow as a result of the life you are leaving. We bring all types of events and experiences in our lives to some closure point although not every life event so neatly ties itself up like death which frankly one can never get over. But overseas, life and the way you lived it, and the thoughts and dreams and person you became because of it, can and should be discussed and validated to allow something new to begin. Without closure, you will continue to live in one part of your life while trying to get on with the next.

2. *Chaos and Limbo*

I could be glib and offer up too literal an interpretation of this stage in the cycle, for how many spouses
have come to know too well the chaos of a packup,
shipments, organising everyone's flight schedules and
arrivals on the other end, and the limbo stage while
you wait for shipments to arrive, visits to customs
inspectors, searching for new housing and on and on
it goes!

But in this context, chaos and limbo are both emotional and practical concepts. You exist in a no man's
land, a zone which is neither one of comfort nor security, when you become caught in the waiting game
and must rely on extraordinary skills in exercising
patience for life to sort itself out again. In short, this
is the stage when you are no longer overseas but not
yet settled 'home' again. You are en route, visiting
friends and family, staying in a hotel while house
hunting, or even into your new home using borrowed
plates and cutlery. Your new life is out there, but
can't begin until everyone is settled and it falls to the
wife and mother to leave herself to last in that department. So you feel, depending on the time of day, tired,
euphoric, optimistic, pessimistic, happy, sad, up and
down, anything but stable for longer than a few minutes or maybe, if you are lucky, a few hours at a time.
This is the stage when I typically rent a lot of videos
or hole up in a movie theatre if possible to escape
from my own brain which won't stop ticking over.
I'm waiting. I'm hoping.

3. *Period of Reconnection*

I am painting broad strokes here (and in later chapters will fill in some of the gaps) because in between

chaos and the period of reconnection will come all sorts of mini-stages. But in the larger context, this third stage of reconnection represents when you finally settle down, move out of the chaos stage and into the comfort zone of being happy to be back. It's when you know what you are going to do, watch your children happily go off to school with their friends, and your partner leave for the office without that worried look on his face that while he's out you are going to curl into a ball on the couch and not move until everyone comes home.

This period of reconnection *does* finally arrive. For the lucky ones, it may take as little time as three to six months; for others a year or two. The eighteen month mark seems to be a particularly popular turning point but I do know women who say it took them as long as five years. It doesn't matter how long – the point is that you *will* feel connected again (even if you don't believe it right now).

Enjoy Every Last Minute

During a speaking tour through old Asian haunts while I was writing this book, I was often asked if there was anything I should have done in say, Beijing, that I didn't and might regret. Buy more furniture! That, of course, is my own glib reply to a serious question (although I actually do kick myself for not buying more Chinese furniture).

When I would turn serious on the matter, as I am now, I would tell my audiences to enjoy every last minute of their overseas sojourn. It's true there are daily expat issues to cope with, husbands away, children who can't settle and so the list goes on. But in the real world of home (and that's definitely how I differentiate my two experiences) all of those regular every day issues will be there, only heightened by so many others, like mortgages, homeowning, elderly parents, and taxes, among others. So take advantage and be grateful for the unique privilege you have to live abroad. Soon enough, the responsibilities you may have been running away from, will return in full measure. And remember that the sweet pleasures of being home will come back too.

An Important Challenge Lies Ahead

If you are vigilant about understanding the emotional dynamics of your move as much as the practicalities (that is, how normal your ups and downs are) you can do your best to keep them in check by knowing that bad moods and uncertain days will pass. Absolutely everyone needs time to get used to change. So be sure to give yourself enough of it. Remind yourself of all the good things which lie ahead and above all else, like my swami advised me, think only positive thoughts.

As you read this, you may be embarking on, or are already engaged in, what is officially called re-entry. In truth, it is really a time for entry into the next chapter of your life. Like a good book that takes time to get into, just keep reading.

WHAT IS RE-ENTRY SHOCK?

IT'S THE SHOCK OF BEING HOME

"I was convinced I was rapidly entering a state of Alzheimer's. I couldn't remember things, I was emotionally fragile, and felt as if I didn't exist. I barely knew who I was."
> – A 55-year-old Canadian woman
> comments on her re-entry shock.

I was on an errand at the mall, one that should have been completed without any hitches and allow me to return home quickly to unpack more moving boxes. But in the early days of re-entry, even the easiest task can turn on a dime into a Monumental Trauma.

The chore which led to this particular ordeal involved the local telephone office which, in my part of the world, is unfortunately situated in a shopping mall, a surefire location for a meltdown. Over-stimulated by too many consumer goods screaming *buy me* from storefronts and a pounding headache caused by irritating florescent lighting, a mall is the perfect setting for an Alfred Hitchcock horror movie. The mundane becomes monstrous. And what could be a more ordinary, every day task than hooking up a new telephone?

According to my endless *to do list,* I could no longer postpone ordering up the telephone lines to accommodate all of our new technology, purchased in a fog with *flying money,* and unopened in boxes stashed in a corner until I worked up the courage to figure out the instructions.

I wandered around the telephone showroom to check out the latest in phone decor and function as I waited for my number to be called. My eyes glazed over at the sheer magnitude of the selection. Perched atop pedestals, sophisticated track lighting showcasing them like works of futuristic fine art, some telephones boasted features which frankly baffled me.

When I was finally called to the customer wicket, my problem turned out not to be with the questions I had jotted down to ask, but with the answers offered by the clerk who had the misfortune to have me as a customer that day. Most of her answers were incomprehensible. It was like being abroad again and knowing little bits of the local language, proudly using them with shopkeepers only to get hit in the face by a stream of words that made absolutely no sense. Overseas, I always received a smile for my efforts. There were no smiles for me on this day as I politely inquired how to go about setting up separate lines for our phone, fax and internet.

Barely looking up from paperwork generated by the previous customer, the phone bureaucrat informed me I would likely require a smart phone for the purpose I had in mind.

"Yes," I answered politely, thinking of the phone art around me, "I would like it to look smart."

"No," said the woman in a voice reserved for children and newcomers to Canada who don't yet speak English, "Not a phone that looks smart. One that acts smart."

"Could you please explain that again?" Tears, an almost daily occurrence at that time, were waiting to pounce behind eyeballs still spinning from my showroom tour. At the same time, self-loathing was working its way into my system. I couldn't believe I was getting so agitated over a stupid telephone.

Her explanation was technical drivel to me. Did I care that telephone lines could magically be split in two and the phone would automatically flip a switch if the caller was in fact a caller or a fax machine, or indeed a long distance caller using a fax machine? My heart started to race and knees to wobble. A panic attack could no longer patiently wait on hold. The clerk began drawing diagrams on the back of an envelope. I became more confused and knew hostility was threatening to overload my emotional switchboard.

Too late. A switch flipped. My panic turned to anger and tears of frustration burst from my eyes. I irrationally decided that blame for this debacle must definitely be assigned to my husband. Why wasn't he here doing this? He was out of town of course, leaving me to deal with repairmen, carpet layers, electricians and general handy guys who now populated my house and were the only people I actually spoke to in the course of the day.

The phone clerk then dealt me the final blow, asking, "And what kind of extra line would you like for your modem?" I started to laugh hysterically. I knew I couldn't hang up on her. She was standing right in front of me. I was in the throes of re-entry shock.

Carlanne Herzog hits it right on the button when she explains that culture shock assails us in both mental and emotional ways.

"Mentally, we are required to cope daily with an incredible number of decisions. We had learned to function in a foreign culture in ways that differed from back home and this only serves to confuse and frustrate still more. Then, in the midst of re-educating ourselves our minds become overloaded. It is a real shock," she says.

What is Re-entry Shock?

Re-entry shock is simply the shock of being home. It's the reverse culture shock you experience in your own country when you visit places that should be familiar to you, but aren't; try to interact with people you should feel comfortable with, but don't; or face situations you should be able to handle, but can't. There can be no simpler way to explain it. Re-entry shock is when you feel like you are wearing contact lenses in the wrong eyes. Everything looks almost right.

These feelings are particularly disconcerting when they happen in your native country and can be far worse than just a bad case of culture shock. Abroad, you expect to feel foreign; you don't expect to when you come home. When this shock does occur as it does for everyone in some form or another it can make you feel extremely unsettled and often, so insecure and inadequate, that it can spark a veritable emotional chain of reactions.

Like culture shock, it has a cycle of its own which must be worked through to its natural conclusion. Depending on various factors discussed in this chapter, re-entry shock can last mere weeks. For others, it may be years before the contact lenses are fitted back into the correct eyes.

Re-entry Shock Can Be Worse for the Spouse

At home with the moving boxes and endless details to attend to, the non-working spouse often feels the blows of re-entry shock harder than the partner who goes directly to an office and structured job, or a child who heads off to school. That's not to dismiss the intensity of shocks for the employee or the child, but they are different from the ones experienced by the spouse.

Isolated, lonely, and exhausted from unpacking or chatting only with real estate agents and the service people helping put a home together, the spouse is left grappling with the harsh realities of re-entry, like starting over again and thinking how nice it would be if a new life could just magically emerge from the moving boxes. Unwrapping reminders of the old life can bring on nostalgic tears borne out of that exhaustion and loneliness. Overly-anxious to get everything settled and get on with life already, the inventory of spousal emotions that emerges at this time can be almost as complex as the list of household belongings. These feelings are similar to the ups and downs associated with the culture shock of a new foreign assignment. That's because at first, home can seem like a new assignment, especially if the re-entry has been into a brand new city.

It's completely natural to feel like a foreigner at first. Though your own culture's cues may be all around, they are still unfamiliar.

Permanent Versus Temporary Re-entry

Have you moved home for good with the intention of staying put and accepting no more overseas assignments? If so, that reasonably describes permanent re-entry. Are you just in between assignments, sometimes for as long as two to four years or for as short a time as one month? Well, that's just as obviously a temporary break from expatriate life. Your reactions to being home and how you go about building your new life will depend greatly into which category your re-entry falls.

For instance, depending on the type of re-entry, there will be very distinct differences in the way you

structure your new life, like finding a home to live in
for a few months or a year instead of a much longer
term. Such differences will impact on how quickly or
how well you adjust. If you have to spend a lot of time,
money and energy house hunting instead of grabbing a
short term rental, the adjustment period may be length-
ened. There will be other decisions which will impact
on your adjustment. Are you going to buy a new car?
Look for a full time job you may have to abandon in
short order? Spend time renovating? Spending money,
money and more money? Getting over spending too
much money upon return is like culture shock too. It
has a definite end. You run out of it!

There will be numerous overlapping emotions
which will be felt in both scenarios. For now, because
there are so many similarities (and especially as they
relate to return shock which I am about to discuss)
I believe readers can find advice and support in the
words I write about either scenario.

What is Temporary Re-entry?

Temporary re-entry is just that: *temporary*. It's not
quite like Home Leave, but you are aware that you
will be leaving again in a few months or years so you
never quite allow yourself to settle in. One foot is
firmly planted outside the door. You will experience
the same cycle as culture shock, but your eye is still
fixed on the airport in the distance and the moving
boxes are never really put away for good.

Temporary re-entry carries its own stressful list of
uncertainties, all of which will contribute to how well
you settle in, even in the short term. When you know
you may leave again (and probably don't even know
when) it's hard to get motivated to set up friendships
or work situations. I like to compare it to not bother-

ing to try to lose the pregnancy weight of your first child when you know a second one will only put it all back on so you decide to wait until you are completely done. It is also another one of those twisted laws of fate that the minute you finally feel settled, your partner will come home and announce you are off again (or wait until you are relaxing on a holiday somewhere to share the 'good news' that you are moving again after only 18 months home, which is how my partner broke to me the news that we were moving to Seoul. Some holiday).

What is Permanent Re-entry?

Permanent means you plan (or hope) to stay put in one place. Either your partner has retired, the children have grown up, you have been retired by force, or any number of the other circumstances I raised earlier may apply. In a permanent scenario, upon coming home you must construct your life differently knowing that the goal is to settle down, the exact opposite of an expatriate constantly on the move. There will be different issues that crop up especially for the spouse (most certainly if you have been away for a long period of time) and they will slowly creep into your life.

From my own experience, permanent re-entry is the much bigger emotional challenge, although I would like to state for the record that I have never trusted my partner as far as I can throw him when it comes to the overseas life, so I should remind myself that nothing is permanent or forever. Just the word *permanent* itself can sound ominous, like the situation is written in indelible ink and can never be rewritten.

When you always had one foot out the door, it didn't matter as much if something didn't work out because you always knew in the back of your mind that you could escape the bad job, the bad neighbour, the local bully annoying your child, or the family member who was driving you crazy. Upon re-entry and especially from an assignment that was not a favourite, you feel the opposite. You feel you have escaped from something. So when the re-entry is supposed to be permanent, and you suddenly realise there is no escape, the challenges can be enormous because you will want to make the place you have returned to, the one place you never want to leave. Easier said than done.

Stages of Re-entry Shock

A person grappling with re-entry shock will experience the same cycle as the culture shock of moving abroad. One very significant difference is that the shock of returning home, especially if it does happen to be for good, can often last a lot longer. Gone is the accelerated pace of expatriate life where in two years you could jam in a lifetime of experience and friendship. Going home, things move slower. A lot slower. Some of the stages may last longer, prolonging the time period between arrival and the time you reach a comfort zone of community and connections. What are those stages?

The Honeymoon Period

The honeymoon period (the one I believe spouses can sometimes miss if they blink) is the best part of any move and especially the one which takes you home. At the time of re-entry, you are thankful for even the smallest things, like the local department store that sells underwear in your size made with 100% cotton. Life is viewed through those proverbial rose-tinted glasses.

The morning after moving into our new North Vancouver home, my partner and I took a walk through the rain forest next door. After polluted Seoul, I felt like I was entering an oxygen tent thanks to the tallest trees I had ever seen in my life. I felt dizzy as we headed for our 'perfect little village' where I would be introduced to the west coast with my first taste of a Starbucks latte. Staring directly out at the mountains, sipping coffee so loaded with caffeine I felt even more lightheaded, it was the perfect honeymoon moment.

If your move goes smoothly, if shipments arrive as they should, houses purchased without major coronaries occurring over price, and everyone seems to be happy to be home, enjoy the honeymoon period while it lasts. It does come to a crashing end.

The Crisis Stage

The real crisis of re-entry often hits the spouse after everything is unpacked and she doesn't know yet how to fill her day. In the absence of outside stimulation or interaction, she retreats into her own mind, a dangerous place littered with memories, expectations, and fantasies that belong only in Hollywood.

My own crisis stage obviously occurred around the time I was crying in that phone store incident I described earlier. Margaret, an American acquaintance who spent a total of thirteen years as an expat, remembers well when her honeymoon ended. After her son was at school for about a week (he started midwinter which can be tough enough), the school informed her that he needed to have a skin test for tuberculosis. Testing positive due to exposure Margaret believed occurred while they were living in Hong Kong, the situation was reported to the local health authorities who monitored her son for six months with letters, calls and follow ups.

"I felt like an alien in my own country," Margaret told me. "Like we were a contaminated family. I felt so foreign and rejected. I was clearly past honeymoon and into anger. We had only been back three weeks."

Certainly there can be many other factors contributing to a crisis: a retired husband underfoot too much of the time, a sick parent demanding all of your time, or a new city or circumstances.

But when your partner tells you that your shock is all in your head, he's sometimes not that far off the mark. (Please don't tell my partner I said that). A crisis of confidence, an identity or mid-life crisis, even a crisis of conscience (did we move to the right place for our children?) are just some of the emotional dilemmas which can drive the spouse up and down the mood scale day in and day out during this stage. She is simply thinking too much.

Unhappy in the early days home, you may wonder (or be asked by your partner who reminds you how unhappy you also claimed to be overseas) if you are, in fact, capable of being happy anywhere at all. You rationalise constantly. You like yourself one minute and despise yourself the next for being so weak and useless. You think about looking for work and then wonder if anyone could possibly want to hire you. You hate yourself for not being more grateful for the wonderful experience you had abroad and then quickly blame that same experience for putting you in this present pickle. In short, it's the ultimate bad hair day that you feel will never ever go away. Remember though: this too will pass.

Period of Readjustment and Reconciliation

There is no finer moment than the day you wake up and feel you truly are home. I hate to use pregnancy analogies too often, but I vividly recall the day my morning sickness while carrying my son just lifted from me and blew away, mercifully after only ten weeks of pregnancy. I felt the same exhilaration when I felt my return shock finally lift. I can't pinpoint the exact moment it left me, but I do recall the thought process (and the all important time frame) from which I was able to bring it to its natural conclusion.

I started to feel connected, not just to my community but more importantly to myself, around the two year mark. In talking to others, this seems to be a roughly common time zone —18 months to three years for a complete return to normal (whatever that is). For some, feeling connected may come with the first paycheque received for work finally secured. For me, after two years or so, enough time had passed between Seoul and Vancouver; some history had been built in my community (I could remember when a building was not in my village or I could return for my second annual medical appointment); and I started to make eye contact with people who seemed familiar to me. Professionally, I was still floundering on the shores of a rocky reinvention, but my life has always been that way anyway so I didn't put as much emphasis on it.

I reached a *period of reconciliation*. Reconciliation is one of the natural conclusions of a mid-life crisis, a life stage which can definitely be kicked into gear when you make a major change in your life in your late thirties or forties. You grow up, you move on, you get past it. It's important to just pick a phrase that describes the process whereby you stop worrying about what will happen next and begin to take each day as a gift.

It was as simple as this: I just woke up one day and realised I had more or less put the pieces of my life back together. I often compare my life to a Chinese plate dance (where the dancer juggles half a dozen plates in the air in perfect balance). If I am missing even one plate, the rest fall down. When I reached my period of reconciliation, it was because I knew my life was once again balanced. I had found my plates again (and they were not all necessarily the plates I wanted but I had accepted them) and I was dancing happily with all of them held high in the air again. I no longer was furiously opposing the circumstances of my life. The fighting inside my head stopped. Should I be here or there? Should I be angry at my husband or grateful for the exotic life his job provided us with? Should I look back with bitterness or move forward with optimism? All that questioning finally ceased. The inner disputes and turmoil were finally reconciled. It's a wonderful moment because you finally find inner peace by silencing the screaming in your head.

"Making Sense of Life's Changes"

Author William Bridges, a transition guru who doesn't have to grow a beard or sit atop a mountain top to gain anyone's respect, writes about the ambiguous nature of transition. In the early pages of his first book to help people make sense of change in their lives, *Transitions: Making Sense of Life's Changes*, he writes: "There are ways of facilitating transitions … and they involve developing new skills for negotiating the perilous passage across the 'nowhere' that separates the old life situation from the new. But before that can be done, you need to understand your own characteristic ways of coping with endings."

Non-judgmental, Bridges points out: "Everyone finds endings difficult, so your own style is not a sign that you have some 'problem' that others don't have. Both the person who leaves early and the one who stays late are avoiding endings and the discomfort of facing the fact that there is a break of some sort in the continuity of things."

"However you learn to deal with them," writes Bridges, "endings are the first phase of transition. The second phase is a time of lostness and emptiness before 'life' resumes an intelligible pattern and direction, while the third phase is that of beginning anew."

Bridges wasn't even writing about re-entry shock, but his three stages of transition could well describe its cycle. The 'nowhere' stage, the lost and empty time which he describes, can definitely be compared to the crisis stage in the re-entry cycle.

To help you get to the good part, the readjustment, his point about 'endings' should probably not go unheeded. How did you end your expatriate experience? Was there unfinished business left hanging? Likewise, how have you handled other endings in your life? Denial? An overly-long grief period? Bridges wisely points out that the manner in which you handle times of transition (in this case, re-entry) may very well mirror how you handled other endings in your life. Are there valuable lessons lurking in your own previous experience?

Re-entry and Life's Muddle

There are more lessons to be learned from other parts of your life. For instance, this is a good point to mention that re-entry shock often gets muddled up with life and its many passages. If you move home at the age of 40 and suddenly question the meaning of your life, are you confused because you are 40 and like half the human race, experiencing a mid-life crisis right on schedule? Or are you mixed up because you are 40, just returned from living in foreign countries for 15 years or more, and have to figure out a new life in a new town?

There is no correct answer to those questions because the truth overlaps, usually against the physically, emotionally shaky and often unrecognisable person you have temporarily become. To cope and eventually get over your shock, it's necessary to separate the life issues from the culture shock issues as best you can. That is, ask yourself, would you have the same feeling about whatever issue is facing you if you had never lived abroad and returned?

Just to be clear, however, there are distinct symptoms impacting on the spouse which will help you truly know you are in return shock and help you make some of those separations.

What Can Heighten Re-entry Shock Waves?

Lest anyone think only a mid-life crisis can heighten feelings of return shock, let me set that notion straight. I did a re-entry workshop for young Canadian ESL teachers who spent time away in Japan as part of an international program called JET (Japan Exchange Teaching) and found they too were suffering from reverse culture shock brought on by some life issues I certainly came to believe are universal beginning with:

Family Expectations

For younger people who move away at the beginning of their careers, returning home and facing parents who now expect them to get on with their 'real' lives and marry, or at the very least, settle down, is a confusing experience. I am convinced that family members are pathologically incapable of understanding what another family member is doing (ever heard your life described to someone by a sibling or a cousin?) This means that upon coming home, a young person (not unlike a more mature older person) must face precisely the issues they may have left the country to avoid. A bad economy or lack of opportunity may force some young people abroad to teach English but eventually they have to return and figure out how to make a living. Panic sets in and can be fuelled by family expectations and reminders that time marches on, they have had their overseas adventure, and now they have to get on with life.

Likewise, family expectations heaped on the older returnees can make life equally difficult. If you have delayed having more children until you were home, parents may be telling you to get on with it and give your child some siblings. If your parents are older, you may now be expected (not asked) to step in and look after a sick parent. Family may demand your presence at all family functions even if you only live half way across the country now instead of halfway around the world. Many family members will never *ever* believe that overseas life represented any hardship whatsoever. Do not expect them to change their minds once you are home. Instead of arguing about it, save your breath for the more important challenges facing you.

Employment Expectations

If re-entry has taken place to support the spouse's wishes to get herself established again on some mean-

ingful career path (and if this doesn't happen overnight which would be the exception and not the rule)
then all the emotional land mines of re-entry will
definitely blow up in your face.

Career-minded spouses who moved abroad to support a partner's career usually want to immediately
jump back into the work force upon re-entry. If that
doesn't happen, the energetic, power-suited person,
with new cell phone and briefcase in hand, and new
business cards at the ready will be replaced with that
miserable wretch lying comatose on the couch. De-
moralised from sending out hundreds of résumés or
making phone calls that go unanswered, self-esteem
is plummeting like the rain from the storm clouds.
Business judgement may be equally cloudy. In the
meantime, on the subject of expectations about work,
consider this perverse and sadly true scenario:

Less than a month after our arrival in Vancouver
(as my partner was shoving me out the door) I landed
a meeting with an executive then heading the Vancouver International Airport Authority. Even though I
was so unbelievably far from ready to meet anyone
and speak coherently (that is, I didn't know yet what
I wanted to do, just that I wanted to do something –
not the smartest employment strategy) I was thrilled
to be called in for a chat based on my résumé. Vancouver airport had expanded enormously and no pun
intended, was really taking off. This energetic, highly
respected and charismatic airport authority president
seemed genuinely excited to meet someone with my
unique qualifications, specifically my ability to get
up and travel anywhere by myself. The meeting went
so well, that a month later, contract in hand, I was
shipped off on what I thought would be the first of
many dream assignments: I was sent to Miami, Flor-

ida of all places (which at the time was a new destination for flights from Vancouver) to spend a week, at their expense, writing a magazine supplement. I tried hard to overlook the fact that it was a long way from Seoul to Miami after just three months home. I just kept my eye on the task at hand instead of hiding under the hotel bed and worrying about being mugged in a Miami taxi.

I was convinced that I had finally met the right person at the right time and this was going to be my easiest reinvention ever. The scenario would lead me to expect that, right? Wrong. The week in Miami was wonderful (getting away from home and unfinished unpacking being the best part) and I dutifully turned in a ten thousand word supplement for which I was paid extraordinarily well. Then ... total silence. I was never to meet the president again, nor could I ever reach by telephone a vice-president who had handled the assignment with me. Had I imagined all of it? That was when that miserable wretch of a woman emerged to take up her position on the couch, waiting for phone calls that were never returned, naively shocked that people could be so mean and rude.

Finally, (because this story has to have a conclusion), here it is: When I showed up at the airport for a meeting that was eventually set up after more than four months, an interminable time period in which I was kept dangling on that precipice with obscure promises of more work, I was stood up! I was so insignificant (the part of the story where my self-esteem took a nuclear blast) that the individuals didn't even turn up for the meeting. I was devastated.

Recounting this degrading incident later to a friend, and describing how half-crazed with anger and disappointment I had been when nobody turned up for the scheduled meeting, I ran into the airport parking lot in the pouring rain in search of my car, tears streaming down my face, contemplating turning around and boarding any plane to get me out of town my girlfriend dryly commented: "You know, Robin, I think your life needs theme music."

The lesson I learned was simple: Manage your expectations wisely but don't expect your professional life to work out easily. Sometimes, you need to hit rock bottom. Fortunately, the only way to go from there is up.

My girlfriend's one liner about theme songs restored my perspective (that is, my sense of humour) and put my expectations into their proper place. There are no dream scenarios, at least not for us ordinary mortals, and if there are, don't expect dreams to come true quickly. I would not have shared that enormously humiliating experience if I didn't want to stress the importance for other career-minded hysterical spouses to put their own career expectations into their proper place or risk making what will already be a difficult re-entry period, worse. Melodramas are clearly fun to write about after the fact, but perfectly dreadful at the time.

Your Partner's Expectations

For the spouse, the absolute worst expectations in my experience can come from the working partner. These can be a mixed blessing. When I asked Eva, a Canadian friend now in her sixties, whose husband retired after serving many times as an ambassador if she was getting support at home, she wrote me: "He's always been supportive!" But then she added: "He's also always had unreasonably high expectations on my behalf!"

seemed dangerous. All of us were nervous and desperately in need of a forum in which we could put our feelings out on the table. So we would have a family meeting after dinner together where we brought out the talking bottle and passed it to each of us individually. Whoever held the bottle could spill out the contents of their minds. It was amazing what came out the first time we did it: My husband expressed his anxiety about my ability to cope with another move; I expressed my fears of taking the kids to a place where war could break out; my son worried about our airplane being shot down (although he thought he was moving to Bosnia at the time, don't ask how that confusion came about); and my daughter? She was concerned that the hotel we would stay in until our permanent quarters were ready would be undergoing renovations (as it had been during a visit we once made there and which she obviously remembered). She was worried I would literally go off my head with frustration. Honesty can be humorous to be sure, but each of us were able to reassure the others in the family and everyone got up from the dinner table feeling a whole lot better. I heartily suggest one family meeting before you leave your post and once again, soon after your arrival at 'home.'

Friends Friends Friends

Children don't like to leave behind friends and the thought of trying to make new ones can make their guts wrench, especially during teen years when friends are a central factor in their lives. As a parent, you need to be front and center not only in helping to facilitate new friendships but maintaining the old ones left behind.

Before leaving our last post, I remember so well how my daughter fretted that she would never see her friends again. Keeping in touch would be entirely her responsibility, I told her, but I made sure the technology she needed to do that was put into place to help her. Then, I encouraged her to learn how to use it.

Facilitating new local friendships rather than e-mail ones, is a lot harder. Early school days will be tough while your child struggles for admittance into new groups. Kids can be terribly mean and very exclusive. They will simply ignore someone new, especially at a large school. As for the new kid, if he or she has had such a different childhood on top of everything else, it will be hard for them to integrate, especially if language skills are an impediment. Talk to your school counsellors or teachers early on. Take your child with you on at least one of those meetings preferably before school begins for the year so they don't fret about what lies ahead. Ask the school officials about neighbours who might have children the same age or find out if there are other new kids who may feel as lost as your own.

It's easier to help younger children make new friends because unlike teenagers, they don't mind if their mother hovers in the background. This will not be the case with teenage children who would rather be seen with Attila the Hun than their mother. The only advice I can offer is to try to think back to when you were a teenager.

Teaching Children About Rights and Responsibilities

Children need to be made aware that there are actions they can and need to take all by themselves. You have to teach them, though, and I personally don't believe children are ever too young to discuss the importance of taking charge of their lives. When introducing them to the delights and freedoms offered at home in your own societies, the first lesson should be that along with those rights also come responsibilities. This idea extends both into the world at large and into the new home you are creating.

Too often when living overseas, our lives are out of our control. Companies decide when a move takes place, embassy staff or realtors look after home repairs, travel agents arrange holidays, family back home line up appointments for Home Leave: the list of life tasks assigned and carried out by others while living as expatriates can go on and on. For many expats, there always seemed to be someone around to do whatever task needed doing. Like their parents, children can be in for major shocks when confronted with the real do-it-yourself world at home, where there is no maid to pick up clothes or wash the dinner dishes. Life's challenges and tasks have to be faced head on at home, and often that can be as overwhelming for a child as it is for an adult.

Whether it's cleaning their room, washing up after dinner, ironing, taking out the garbage, painting the new fence, or starting a new club at school, children who have enjoyed the expatriate existence may now have to learn to do things for themselves. I have heard more than one expat parent fret that their college-bound student would likely end up living in a room full of dirty clothes because the concept of operating a washing machine would baffle him or her.

Our children have the skills to meet the challenge of taking personal responsibility for their lives. They have returned home open-minded, tolerant, and holding a global view that allows them to know even at a basic level that they are in the world's lucky minority. To demonstrate how grateful they are to be so privileged, they need to be reminded how important it is to be socially responsible, to give something back to their world. As they are also flexible, adaptable and in possession of life skills that make them special regardless of how they may now feel about their uniqueness, they just need to rearrange their strengths to meet their new reality.

Parents can't make new friends for their children, but they can reinforce (and remind them) of their past successful performance in the friend-making department. The family may no longer enjoy the services of domestic household help, but children can be taught the importance of helping to keep the family home clean and in order. Bought your son a bicycle which he can ride safely in your new neighbourhood? Teach him how he can stop and pick up milk or bread for you while he's out cruising around or be thoughtful enough to ask if you need anything.

Most important of all, is your son or daughter whining again (however legitimately) about feeling homeless and disengaged from the local culture? Show them by example not only how to become engaged in their new community (through clubs or associations for instance) but explain why it is important to take these steps. For instance, your child may have been engaged overseas in some wonderfully socially beneficial volunteer work. Now comes the opportunity for you to show them why they should become as enthusiastically involved in helping alleviate some of the social problems of their own communities. Take them to the local food bank or shelter. Give them an eyeful of truly homeless people. And take a good look yourself while you are there. I had to do this myself on more than one occasion.

Keep Parental Travel To a Minimum If Possible

The tensions associated with a move, as all veteran expatriates know, can be difficult enough, but making them even worse is when one parent is away for what seems like a good chunk of the time. This is not an unusual situation upon re-entry. The working partner often returns to headquarters or a new position which wants to capitalise on his or her ability to work in the international marketplace. Well, the marketplace requires a plane to get there and takes that working partner away from home. How often and indeed how far away will depend on the job.

If the family is prepared for this phenomenon, life will go much smoother. A partner may still be absent and place the burden of the adjustment period on you, but you won't be surprised by it and you can likely prepare for it by hiring additional help or begging family to assist. You may also avoid taking steps which can only make matters worse.

Take our border collie. Please take our border collie! Our former family pet, a beautiful four year old Shetland sheepdog, had died unexpectedly in Seoul two months before our re-entry, a heart wrenching situation I would never want to live through again. Our children, we promised, would have a new dog to cuddle the minute we moved home or soon after. So without thinking of breeds or any of other logical planning which should go into the choice of a family pet, we rushed out and got our border collie. Too bad we didn't stop to think it through. It definitely qualified as one of those instant decisions you make upon coming home, like buying a house or a car or curtains all on the same day. You are just too over-whelmed to give it the proper attention.

Border collies need to work, and on that score, I commiserated with the pooch I was trapped with all day, watching him herd my furniture in the absence of any cattle in my living room. He needed a lot of exercise, especially a good run, and I don't run. This was something father and daughter had decided to do together. But the father was never there! Border collies are the smartest canine breed, a brilliance I be-lieve they use for evil. He also requires an alpha wolf to lead his pack and take orders from. Our daughter, barely five feet at the time, was not tall enough to play this role although she tried very hard.

I may just be writing about something as simple as the family pet, but the mistake we made is illustra-tive of the kind it is so easy to rush into upon re-entry because we are desperate to create some sem-blance of order for the family. What could be a cosier picture? New house, new neighbourhood and new puppy. The problem was, we were not ready for a new dog (we were still grieving the one who died). We could have used a transition period, yet we went out and got him without doing all the proper re-search and without recognising the impact of my part-ner's travel on the dog's behaviour which in turn, im-pacted profoundly on us. As a result, our early days became so much harder than they needed to be.

If my partner's constant travel was tough on the dog, imagine the havoc it wreaked with my son Ja-mie's adjustment. Like clockwork, the day after his father would go away, my son would feel sick and want to stay home from school. He missed his father and didn't like the unsettled feeling he got when his father went away all the time. Guilt-ridden about his travel, my husband didn't want to hear any of this. He was too busy coping with his own re-entry shock and adjustment, a subject I will get to in a minute.

When Your Child Has Difficulty Adjusting

If six months or even a year goes by and your child is still resisting going to school, making new friends, joining teams, or any other overt signs of not settling down, consider seeking professional help. Before racing off to a psychologist, though, start with your own family doctor. (If moving home has meant having to find a new doctor, this will give you a good excuse to find one). In all likelihood there will be nothing medically wrong with your child but rule all physical possibilities out. If medically speaking your child is sound and hearty, consider psychological counselling and do it sooner rather than later. There may be all sorts of issues building inside their brain which you can't penetrate and the longer they are allowed to fester, the harder they will be to sort out. If you do decide to go down the route to the psychologist, make sure that your counsellor has experience of third culture children before you go.

The other questions to consider are similar to those you may ask of yourself: is a child's behaviour (like your own) a product of the re-entry experience? Or is it muddled up with other life issues? If you returned home minus a parent either through divorce or death, could that be driving your child's unhappiness? Could your child be responding to your own unhappiness? Is your child acting up as a way of getting your attention? Is your child a teenager? Enough said. If you feel you cannot come up with the answers to those questions, it's time to bring in professionals.

The Working Partner's Re-entry Shock and How It Affects the Family

I mentioned at the outset of this book that it is not my intention to get into serious number crunching of how many repatriated employees quit their jobs on return. Nor am I going to delve into what corporations or governments should be doing about re-entry except where their intervention with programming or support might help the family's transition. When I do get an opportunity to speak to corporations about the needs of the family upon repatriation, I point out that an employee who is worried about the home front is neither a productive nor loyal employee.

The working partner's re-entry shock is important to me for one very simple reason: an employee unhappy in the work place, will not be a happy spouse or parent at home and that will impact on the resettling of the entire family.

To keep this discussion simple, I have divided the working partners into two succinct categories:

Employees Who Go Home To No Job

This heading is multi-purpose because it covers employees who may return to no paying job at all (if they have been downsized, considered redundant or retired altogether) or who do return to their corporate or government headquarters with barely an office, never mind a job description to call their own. This latter situation can often be the hardest because it isn't clear cut. Retirement or being out of a job means plans can be made for the next step. But drifting around corporate headquarters, feeling isolated or worse, worthless after several years abroad with chauffeur driven cars and other perks of expat life, would be hard on anyone's ego. It can be completely debilitating for many who return to find their overseas experience doesn't count zip.

At the end of the day, that same driftless employee returns home to find domestic bedlam: moving boxes piled up, kids complaining they have no friends, and a spouse ready to get to work too but restrained by family commitments and of course, ready to shoot the working spouse. Nobody is adjusting very well. Discussions about everything from money to schools escalate too easily into arguments. The working partner understandably feels overwhelmed by responsibilities. He (or she) wants to speak about the challenges settling in at work but the last person who wants to hear about them is the spouse at home with the painters. Marriage and family counselling may be called for, but everyone is too shocked to know where to look for it and reluctant to admit it may be needed.

This is the point where companies can and should intervene with workshops and employee assistance programs and in particular, marriage counselling. But the employee must ask for these services as typically they will not be offered. If the employee says nothing, it will be assumed that the transition is going fine.

Just as common, though, is the situation where an employee knows he needs help but is reluctant to ask for it. It's similar to being overseas and not wanting to admit any problems for fear of looking weak. For the good of the family, though, employees should ask for re-entry assistance if the family is not adjusting. An employee can't function at his job if he is too distracted by problems on the home front. In other words, when it's a choice between some form of corporate assistance or loss of revenue to the company's bottom line, it's amazing how quickly assistance will be rendered.

The partner who has retired can also be a draining experience for a 'shocked' repatriated spouse. My friend Dee in Australia found the stress of her re-entry was definitely compounded by a husband who not only had nothing to do with his time, but resented her finding new interests outside the home.

Partner Who Goes Home to A New Job

This category I know about very well for my partner brought us home because of a new job altogether that couldn't have been any more exciting and challenging. Of course in theory I was thrilled for him, but it didn't take long to want to throw him out the window every time I heard about some other fascinating new opportunity he was engaged in while I watched the new puppy run in circles around the house. When a new job keeps taking the partner away from the family, either with travel commitments, intensive training period, or late nights at the office, the transition period can drag on because it is fuelled by resentment.

Making matters worse in our household was the working partner's guilt about not being around. My children, recognising their father's feelings, walked on egg shells when he was home and tried to never raise the topic of his travel for fear of setting off an argument. This meant that he was either away on a trip, or home not talking about going away on another trip. When travel is the topic on everyone's mind but the words have to die in the throat and never be communicated, it can lead to family tension that you can cut with a knife. The same holds true for the challenges facing employees as they try to settle into new jobs and resettle their families at the same time.

It took us a while, but we finally faced up to our new situation to the point where we could talk about it openly. I vowed to become a born again spouse and not get angry over my husband's travel. For his part, he recognised the family had to talk openly about the impact his new job was having on our home (and that nobody was criticising him for having a good job). My partner regularly e-mails the children when he is travelling and the minute he returns home, he jumps right into fatherhood barely shaking off his jet lag. Getting over that hurdle, I can safely say, was one of the first signs that our family was finally getting over re-entry shock.

Working Partner Needs to Build a New Life, Too

The work place and its impact on family life is only one area where the working partner may be in for a few shocks. Like everyone else in the family, he or she also has to build a new network of friends and interests at home. If distracted by a new job, or exhausted from looking for work, the settling in period – the time when he or she too will feel isolated and often depressed – can drag on for years. Expatriate communities are very self-contained and the cross-over between work and play is easy. That not may be the case at home and the working partner needs to understand the importance of getting out into the new community in order to make a new life. The non-working partner must ensure that time is set aside, without commitment to the family or household chores, for the working partner to get out there and have a life. Everyone will be happier for it.

Third Culture Families

Researchers haven't yet identified any social sub-group known as a 'third culture family'. But with the increasing mobility of a global work force, and more writers and researchers examining the long term effects of our lifestyle, it's only a matter of time before we are legitimised as a unique family grouping. Our children are third culture kids, often feeling like they belong everywhere and nowhere as a result of moving around. We, the parents, are in many ways third culture adults, even though our overseas and cross-cultural experiences may have happened long after we had grown up. The next logical assumption is that together, we become a third culture family.

We certainly don't need to check our passports to know what our first culture is. I used to find just stepping aboard a Canadian airplane, even if it was sitting on a tarmac in Tokyo, could make me feel like I was stepping into a piece of home. And we know and appreciate the secondary cultures we have been exposed to along our peripatetic life adventure. But a third common 'expat' family culture definitely emerges from the combination of the first two, for how else to explain what happens when we find ourselves in a room with another expatriate family? Regardless of what part of the world another family has been living in, there is an instant familiarity and comfort which comes from the shared experience of moving as a family. It takes just minutes for members of one third culture family to hit it off with their opposite numbers even if the meeting takes place – as it so often does – in an airport waiting lounge, hotel lobby, or even on board a thirteen hour flight.

Pollock comments: "It is indeed a unique experience to be a family that is neither like their home country nor the country in which they have been living. They have, indeed, formed a 'third culture.'"

Re-entry Shock is a Family Affair

Considering how close we become in the moving process, family re-entry shock is inevitable, just as family culture shock occurred in the move abroad. Re-entry shock can be not only one individual's reactions to being home, but also a collective experience in which one family member's shock impacts on the others. Too often, it is the accompanying spouse whose shock needs to lift in order to allow everyone else in the family to calm down and enjoy being 'home'.

The bonus offered by mobility is the positive enrichment of family life through travel and shared cultural experiences. More than anything else, the challenges of being home are to ensure your family continues to enjoy each other's company, to learn from each other, to support one another, to become active members of your new communities, and to continue to seek out and appreciate all that life has to offer.

FOUR

SO YOU THINK YOU ARE EXHAUSTED?

FATIGUE, DEPRESSION AND RE-ENTRY SHOCK

*"In the early months after our return, on some days
I felt overwhelming energy and optimism. On others,
I was overwhelmed with fatigue. I sort of alternated
between these two states."*

> – Eva, sixty-something Canadian
> returnee explaining how she felt.

As an over-stimulated person, sort of a Tasmanian Devil hyped up on caffeine, I am well aware that my enthusiastic engagement with life can wipe people out. My high speed conversations often leave people mopping their brows, relieved for the respite when I exit a room.

Moving into the laid back and mellow North American west coast culture (of which Vancouver is the Canadian epicenter) I worried that my high energy, combined with a passion for long-winded outrage (doesn't matter what the subject), were qualities that might not allow me to fit in easily. Would I be able to assimilate into a culture whose natives become passionate over a home delivery from the local organic vegetable market? The fact that coffee houses would be as ubiquitous as the rain presented me with a sidebar conundrum to contemplate. How is it possible to be so laid back while drinking café lattes all day?

It turns out my worries were groundless. My energy just didn't make it back with our shipment from Korea. The Tasmanian Devil was lost at sea.

Fatigue and Depression are NOT Universal Reactions

Let me say this at the outset: some returning spouses feel neither fatigue nor depression upon re-entry. In fact, some women I have spoken to about this felt bursts of energy, not a lack of it; or like my Canadian friend, Eva, whom I quoted at the very beginning, flip flopped between states of energy and fatigue. Personally, I fall into the camp of women who in the early months of re-entry admitted they felt tired, lethargic, enervated, unmotivated, and totally depressed.

Carlanne Herzog warns that we should be clear about what the term 'depression' really means.

"While depression is a term that is often used to loosely describe feelings of sadness, crying at the least little thing or not wanting to get out of bed in the morning, *real* clinical depression is far far worse. Clinical depression involves the body, mood and thoughts; the way you eat and sleep, and the way you think about yourself. However, it is not uncommon to experience a 'depressive episode' at the time of repatriation, particularly if the move coincides with a family or health crisis," she says.

The symptoms I mentioned can be common at the time of re-entry. Many are typical physical symptoms of age, stage, and physical health. Throughout this chapter, I will be constantly stressing the normality of these feelings. Many of us who feel tired and depressed upon re-entry worry there is something desperately wrong. We are also loathe to discuss our feelings or even seek professional help when either (especially the latter) would make us feel a lot better.

For those who haven't been lucky enough to breeze through their repatriation with energy and optimism soaring, read on and discover you are not alone. But be sure to keep reading. There is a happy ending to this story.

First Clues

My first inklings that my own mental strength and energy were not quite up to par were definitely archetypal. It was during the delivery of our final batch of moving boxes that feelings of helplessness shuddered through my body and headed straight for my brain, dragging my emotions along with them. My honeymoon stage should technically have still been in effect, but that phase managed to last only slightly longer than a hiccup. Our storage boxes had already been retrieved; an air shipment had also arrived and had more or less been cleaned out; even most of our suitcases were unpacked. *And then the sea shipment arrived.*

Buried amidst wrapping paper (is there a logical reason why one half-used candle requires so much protection?) and numb from head to toe, I cried at the sight of my kitchen table piled high with stuff I either couldn't remember buying or realised we now owned in duplicate or even triplicate. The movers seemed to be hauling in an endless number of boxes. Dumped at my feet like so many mounds of fertiliser, I could never be convinced that a home would grow from their contents.

It wasn't just the sight of boxes that wiped me out. There was my residual energy failure from the so-called holiday on the way back from Seoul. We (that's me and my children minus their father who was already working) had taken a hectic trip home, making stopovers across my huge country for family visits and rituals. I had even forced myself and my children to make it to an annual family fishing trip after only three days home in Canada. I was more fried than the fish we ate for our lunch ashore.

Any fool, I reassured myself, would feel tired. The rationalisation process had begun in earnest.

The Dark, Rainy Days

Skip ahead several months when we were all moved in, boxes unpacked, house painted, and a million other details had been attended to so the children could start their new schools and my road warrior husband could take off in his new career in international marketing. It was finally time to have a serious go at organising my own, new life. But I still felt overwhelmed by a fatigue I was hard-pressed to understand. Soon, its kissing cousin arrived to torture me: a low-level, unexplained sadness and depression. I would lay down on the couch every morning after everyone left for the day, and not move for hours at a time.

How tiring and depressing it was, lying there so utterly self-indulgently, listening to the rain pour down. My mood kept plummeting like the rain drops. Who was this enormously ungrateful stranger inhabiting my body? Where was the person with all that energy? This alien who had snatched my body was counting neither her blessings nor her calorie consumption. Just opening a book seemed out of the question. And why write letters to anyone if it would just depress my friends to hear how badly I was coping?

Our shipment must have been switched with someone else's. Clearly, I had unpacked the wrong wife. I was too tired and afraid to ask anyone for help. I was consumed by pathetic self-pity. And talk about self-loathing! The self-hatred in the air was so palatable it rivalled a convention of skin headed neo-Nazi teenagers.

Finally, I clued in long enough to consider that maybe my feelings were related in part to the culture shock of my own re-entry. Maybe other physical issues were at work too? Maybe, as a friend finally, kindly, advised me, I should re-read my own books?

Moving Burnout and Blues

The 'blues and blahs' I loftily label *cumulative culture shock fatigue* accumulate of their own free will. An intense emotional experience like moving home certainly can trigger this emotional burnout, but it can also be the result of multiple moves or simply one hectic or difficult relocation.

If your kitchen table is overloaded with trinkets, consider that emotional stuff can also build up in your mind. That includes too much energy expended in bursts of manic behaviour putting houses together or even hanging all the pictures in one frantic day. It can also mean there have been too many people who have been strangers, then friends, then close friends you have to say goodbye to, all in the blink of an eye. Ever wonder why it is that when an expat sees a familiar face at an airport, it takes a few minutes to figure out in which context that face is known to them? The brain has to process too many people.doc files crammed into its enormous hard disk.

Many spouses have waited impatiently for the move home, dreamed of it, and possibly idealised it way too much. Then, on the day you realise you finally are home, you dread taking the next step, creating a new life.

So you lie down on the couch and sleep away the day. It's really just the easiest way to run away from all those responsibilities which have quickly replaced the moving boxes as litter on your new landscape. Your children need you. Your husband needs you. Your parents may need you. Your extended family wants a piece of you. Your dog needs you (I had to deal with that too). Too many responsibilities and too little mental energy to cope with them. You conveniently forget that you need to look after yourself too.

So What's Making You Feel So Tired?

Emotional fatigue is both a logical and natural by product of too many years of packing and unpacking your life. A woman has to work up a lot of self-motivated steam if her own inner momentum is going to drive her efforts at establishing a new meaningful life (and that's assuming she's been able to retrieve her self-confidence which may be lying in a gutter somewhere, bruised and battered). As many women can confirm, that momentum, while high when they first return and fuelled by honeymoon adrenaline, can sometimes flip from optimism into dark pessimism a few months after returning.

Once again, I stress that not all women will feel this. Some women feel elated at being home and find a burst of positive energy that seems to last forever. I wish those feelings could be bottled and offered up to the rest of us like some re-entry Viagra pill.

Women who return home with small children young enough to require caretaking duties will naturally be tired because they still exist in the sleep-deprived years of raising youngsters. That exhaustion goes with the territory of child-rearing.

The kind of fatigue I am referring to likely applies more to women in my own age bracket of between 35–55 which is a common age in which the re-entry exercise can occur. But remember this: it is also the age when other life changes kick in. What are some of these life changes?

Empty Nest

Many repatriated wives come home at a time in life when their children are leaving it. Off to college or into the work world they go, and suddenly, they are gone. The home details and volunteer committees at school that kept women so busy overseas, providing connections to the outer world, also suddenly vanish. Now comes the time they may have been waiting for! Kids off at college or starting their own lives; they are living in their own country; life has settled down. But wait: They can't figure out what to do next. Not only is the nest now empty, it's unfamiliar too and needs rebuilding. Like everything else about the expatriate life, empty nest syndrome, a well-documented passage of adulthood, can become exaggerated upon re-entry and depression is not an unnatural symptom of this period.

Parent-Child Relationships

For some returning spouses, children are not just going off to school but are getting married and raising children. Enter Grandma! Convenient babysitter? At the beginning, you may actually want the job for the sheer novelty. But once the honeymoon period of reuniting with children and grandchildren has worn off, a returning spouse trying to figure out her own life may find herself in head-to-head battles with children. New ground rules have to be set.

My Canadian friend Eva returned home to Montreal and said that one of her daughters living there found it "very difficult to be living in the same city as her mother for the first time since leaving home to go to university at the age of 18 which had been some 13 years earlier."

"While my daughter and her consort were very welcoming and supportive with the house hunting and some very good times were had when we first got back, there was a long period of adjustment before the mother in question understood that a certain amount of distance was required to make the relationship between her and her daughter satisfactory," Eva told me.

"Now, almost four years later, we're living comfortably in the same city and I dare say that the fact that her adorable baby son spends two days a week with me has helped the relationship a lot!" As Eva rightly pointed out to me in our correspondence, she believes relationships with adult children is the kind of unexpected problem an older person might have to deal with upon re-entry.

Other repatriates feel compelled to settle old scores with their parents that may have been hidden away by being out of sight and out of mind. After being away for many years, returnees sometimes feel they have to set their parents straight about a few things (pick a theme, any theme) and settle issues which can no longer be left at the airport.

Not Another Professional Reinvention!

Whether it's because the nest has emptied or the bank account has been wiped out by the cost of moving home, women suddenly face yet another professional reinvention. One paycheque is not enough to support the lifestyle to which the family has grown accustomed. Figuring out what you want to be when you grow up yet again may seem like a daunting challenge to many women, and can precipitate the overwhelming fatigue I am referring to in this chapter. When moving overseas in the first place, it is the career issue more than any other which brings on the first major crisis for many women; coming home, employment issues and challenges may also contribute to the exhaustion level.

Perversely, women who find work immediately can also be exhausted and stressed out. Bente, a Danish acquaintance of mine, lucked into what she felt was the perfect job too soon after her family moved home to Ottawa from Geneva. As a result, she reported to me, in all her 20 years of moving it had never taken her so long to get her house in order. But how could she turn down a good job offer when her two sons were attending private schools which required major cash infusions from her end? Even though no professional reinvention was required, some naughty Viking god was having a good time pushing Bente's buttons. Her stress levels eight months later were, by her own admission, over the top.

For many women, fatigue may simply be wrapped up in an overwhelming sense of not having the mental strength to deal with another professional transformation or one that is foisted upon you too early.

Remember the good news: as always with tales of culture shock of any description, you eventually get over it.

Retired or Downsized Husband Underfoot

If re-entry has occurred because of your partner's retirement or downsizing, there will be yet another new dimension added to your return: a husband at home trying to figure out what he's going to do next while you are doing the same and would prefer to do it by yourself, like you have always done. I complained to an Australian friend of mine that my husband travelled too much when we returned. She, on the other hand, wanted to switch places since her husband was around the house all day and she didn't much like it.

Where before, the husband went out the door every morning to his office, it is now you who wants to trot out the door each day to something new and exciting. It's your turn now! Remember that. Don't let his sulking and sudden neediness (which was the case for my friend in Australia) stop you when you finally have a chance to start something new. Ignore him.

Marriage Issues

And how about your marriage? Can it survive re-entry? Worrying about the state of your marriage can sap your energy too. At various steps along the way home, you may be asking yourself that survival question with more seriousness than you have ever given it before. I know more than one woman who got off the plane from the overseas posting and said: "Right, now that I can finally find a lawyer, you're toast pal." Or words to that effect. Some wait a few months until they feel more settled. But anecdotally, at least, there is evidence to suggest that once on terra firma (recognisable ground with divorce lawyers in the Yellow Pages) a woman walks. Of course nothing is stopping a man from fleeing the scene too, and if the marriage weather gets heavy (arguments about money now that benefits but not lifestyle expectations are gone spring instantly to mind), both partners may be making a beeline for the door.

Younger returning expats face other marriage issues, like whether or not to get on with expanding the family. Housing arguments may also crop up since expat housing can be quite lavish thanks to subsidies; not so upon returning to your true age and stage in your financial life. Regardless of age, challenges in the marriage upon re-entry will abound and can be exhausting to face.

As any veteran expat knows, the stress placed upon marriage by the moving exercise can be enormous, so why would anyone expect the move home to be any different in the war between the sexes? I delve into a wife's anger and resentment in Chapter Six so won't go too far into here except to flag the issues as another potential source of fatigue and depression upon return. It also needs to be said that if one or other of the marriage partners just can't get past the anger, a third party such as a family marriage counsellor should be brought into help and sooner rather than later.

Feelings of Alienation and Isolation

Sometimes, feeling alienated and disconnected from your new community can be exhausting. Margaret, my American acquaintance who earlier described her re-entry crisis point, confessed to feeling overwhelming fatigue upon return. I asked her for a quintessential example of her feelings of alienation upon returning to the US at the age of 50. I would paraphrase her words, except the way she wrote it to me seemed too perfect to change:

"I remember a time on the tennis courts," she relates. "Tennis was the location I had chosen to use as a re-entry point to make friends and to re-learn how to function in this previously known environment.

The ladies I was playing with that day had all been, or were, professional women and were currently not employed. They were sharing stories and I tried to join in. I told my story, and while doing so, looked at each of the women. They had that glassed over look as though they were ready to move on and get to something they could relate to. I cut the story short and withdrew into myself. I need interaction to feel connected and there was none. There were was no head nodding or 'ah ha's. There was nothing."

In so much of what I have learned about repatriation, I have heard that returnees feel depressed because they feel they are pushed to the social sidelines because people can't relate to our experiences. Like Margaret, they tell stories only to have people's eyes glaze over. Feeling like you are living on the margins of your society, you will naturally feel alienated and lonely. These feelings can also be depressing and draining.

Feeling 'Out of Focus'

It may be another side effect of having too many experiences locked up in my brain in desperate need of processing, but for years upon re-entry, I fought a terrible inability to focus. It was like I suddenly had developed an attention deficit disorder. Through the haze of my re-entry shock, I could still muster up the attention required to sort out the house repairs, organise my children's activities, and maybe get myself to a family function or two. But when it came to what I was going to do, a butterfly effect came over me. I would seem to get excited over one idea but before the week was out, I moved onto yet another idea which would occur to me. I couldn't linger on the next idea too long either. Then, of course, I would want to take a nap.

It took me more than two years, and a lot of disappointment over ideas I thought I could finally set my sights on, to understand that my lack of focus was definitely connected to my fatigue and depression. Typical of the way we want to get our lives back in working order after re-entry, I was grasping at straws which I hoped would go into a foundation to support my new life. I was desperate to rebuild my life and gain strength from a new structure. But straws, rest assured, are not sturdy enough to support whatever it is you want to build. One of my many mistakes was trying to build my life before I had the physical and mental strength to do so.

In a few pages from now, I will get even more specific about ways to nurture yourself so that your flexibility, resilience, and sense of humour can also be salvaged from the moving boxes.

Mid-Life Identity Crisis

When it occurs overseas, reaction to many of life's primary challenges (like hitting 30 or 40 or even 50) sometimes get sidelined and reality becomes blurred. For example, when we had our first child overseas, we were so caught up in having our daughter in Bangkok that much of the confusion and unsettledness which overwhelmed us we naturally attributed to having a baby in Thailand, far from home and family. Of course our geography was challenging, but like parents since the beginning of time, we were experiencing the heady distractions caused by a first child. In analysing our bewilderment, we placed more emphasis on the Bangkok part of the scenario rather than the baby part which throws any young couple into a tizzy wherever they have one. A life stage got muddled. As a result, what we took for culture shock to Thailand was really culture shock to "first baby. . . in Thailand, far away from family support."

This also can happen with other life stages, notably mid-life issues of identity. These include all the regular suspects and symptoms of a good identity crisis, including letting go of hopes and dreams and all the other psychobabble terms offered up by pop psychologists or Oprah platitudes which typically have a grain of truth to them.

Mid-life is a stage that, like having babies, doesn't recognise borders. It can't stop and say, Oh, I'll just wait until this individual has settled in one place. It can strike, and usually does, anywhere. Unfortunately, for some women, it can hit men overseas and the fallout sometimes comes in the form of a husband having an affair with a local woman. If it hits either you or your partner soon after coming home, its effects may once again get confused with other issues associated with re-entry and not be recognised for what it truly is: a life passage that has to be dealt with like all others.

Putting the expatriate life behind you and setting up again at home can precipitate a mid-life crisis. That's assuming one is not already in progress. It may have been a mid-life crisis in the first instance which brought about the re-evaluation which led to the re-entry. Searching for answers to questions like 'is this all there is?' or 'what do I want to do with the rest of my life?' and all those other existential questions that you either articulate or just feel (sometimes with depression, or, if you are lucky, with exhilaration) can be very tiring to contemplate but part of a completely normal process.

The quest for the answers to those questions can be hampered by physical changes to your body that you may not be ready (or willing) to put into words but definitely feel. For rest assured that for women of a certain age, some of those symptoms associated with fatigue and depression, while expressions of re-entry shock, are rooted in physical causes.

The Big Change: Menopause and its Early Symptoms

So you think you have changed your life by coming home? Do you really think everything is put back into place now that the moving boxes are empty? Well sit back and get ready for what may be the biggest change of all. The Change. *Menopause* or its prequel: *Menopause: The Early Years*.

The popular bible on menopause is *The Silent Passage*. For many women, it stays hidden in a drawer, out of sight, like the denial deep within every woman that she is getting older or t-shirts are just getting smaller. The author, Gail Sheehy, reports that her book is apparently one of the world's most shoplifted books in the world since women are loathe to discuss this issue, never mind turn up at a checkout counter to pay for a book about it.

I had no problems proclaiming my interest in the subject to the world and certainly not to other middle aged women whom I started to accost with the simple question: do you feel tired all the time? A friend visiting on Home Leave from her posting in Bangladesh labelled us The Tired Generation which I think isn't too far from the truth either, although asking any woman a question about energy levels during a hectic Home Leave is probably unfair and terribly unscientific.

Between Sheehy's book and the almost universal answer of yes! to my question about feeling tired, I immediately started to feel better if for no other reason than no longer did I feel I was alone. There could be *physical* reasons for symptoms which people around me were dismissing as merely continued emotional fallout from re-entry. I was definitely in the right age bracket for some of the physical reactions which precede menopause. Even if I had my hormone levels checked on a Monday, that didn't mean that by Wednesday or Thursday of the same week they couldn't dip into the fatigue zone. A woman's body, like her moods, can be like a yo-yo beginning as a teenager when her hormones start charging up. The same thing happens as her functions wind down.

More importantly, just bringing menopause into the discussion helped me, because I knew I wasn't going crazy unlike some of the unfortunate women Sheehey writes about who lived in the 1950's. Upon reaching menopause, many women of that decade were silently carted away to asylums to 'rest' after being diagnosed with nervous breakdowns which for many, Sheehy writes, was nothing more than the onset of menopause.

Menopause, Fatigue and Depression

What I have found significant about raising the subject of menopause at the time of re-entry, has been the lack of its recognition in the adaptation cycle of an expatriate spouse (because this can't be limited to just coming home. Certainly moving abroad at menopause can't be much of a picnic either). To ignore menopause or any health concerns, in my view, is to have your belongings arrive from overseas with the keys to many, but not all, of the trunks.

Sheehy identifies the onset of fatigue and feelings of being 'out of focus' which can arrive in the years leading up to menopause, a time she labels perimenopause. She also identifies other symptoms of this early pre-menopause period, including a low level, unexplained depression. I knew instantly during re-entry that I had been suffering from something hormonal, for how else could I explain feeling sad with the gorgeous scenery, fresh air, and healthy children around me? I also could begin to think back to the two years we had spent prior to that on posting in Seoul. I began to see other signals of changes to my body which I missed the first time around. One hot flush can be an overheated bedroom; two may be due to a heavy nightgown; three, even spread out over several months, may mark the beginning of the change.

Typically, though, upon re-entry and the emotional shakeup which followed, my physical premenopausal symptoms were getting confused with some of my emotional reactions to coming home. As I explained a few pages back, this is not an uncommon muddle which repatriated women may find themselves in.

Having said all of that, I caution women that symptoms do not disappear just because we put a name or reason to them. Menopause can't, unfortunately, be stopped dead in its tracks. But you will feel better knowing that unlike some of the '50's women, you're not ready to be carted away to a mental health institution either. It could be you are ready for Hormone Replacement Therapy, St. John's Wort, or any other prescriptive remedies your doctor may want to start you on.

Sheehy acknowledges in *The Silent Passage* that whether or not depression is a symptom of menopause is a hotly debated topic. She refers to a much-publicized 1986 report published in a Harvard Medical School publication from the Massachusetts Women's Health Study that states that "depression in middle-aged women is associated with events and circumstances unrelated to the hormonal changes that occur at menopause." Sheehy then quotes one of the co-authors of the study as saying in an interview that: "Most women just go straight through menopause, no problems nor irritability."

Cheekily, Sheehy says that if you tried out that last line on a room full of women, a laugh was sure to follow. Following in her irreverent footsteps on this matter, I can personally report advising women's groups when out on speaking tours on the subject of spousal re-entry, "Don't come home until after menopause!!!" Like Sheehy, I am also guaranteed a laugh every time.

Menopause at the Time of Re-entry

It is equally true, however, that repatriated women of a certain age do face a sort of double challenge: our events and unique circumstances, the shock of the changes in our lives at the time of our re-entry may very well precipitate depression at mid-life and then be further compounded by issues of menopause.

Ann Houston Kelley, who writes and speaks about mid-life challenges for women on the move as part of her Netherlands-based company Nomadic Life, confirmed my feelings of a connection between menopause, life abroad, and ultimately, re-entry.

"I think that many women come ' home' during this time of life expecting that it will be great to be closer to family and friends," Ann writes to me, "only to find that this element of the 'context' (that is, menopause, perimenopause, youth-oriented culture in western society) makes the re-entry all that more difficult."

"I don't think that most internationally mobile 'accompanying spouses' really have a choice about when they come home," says Ann. "I do think, though, if menopause and perimenopause make ordinary life more difficult, it can really impact on the potentially difficult process of re-entry."

So how do you "come through the tunnel" (the expression Ann has chosen for the adaptation necessary for mid-life adjustment) into a time of "mastery and integrity," the phase popularised by Sheehy in her follow up bestseller *New Passages?*

"Understanding the issues and sharing information, experiences, and possible strategies for this life stage in an international environment can all help," writes Ann. I couldn't agree more.

The Exciting Part of Life Is Over

In the opening chapter of this book, I shared my own experience of desperately seeking enlightenment in India before our repatriation. I figured like so many others that the interesting part of life would end the minute I stuck my passport in the drawer. Once again, jumbled up with typical mid-life issues and menopause, can be a misguided feeling that life (or is it just youth?) is over now that you have come home. No more exotic trips, dinner parties for 20 that were a snap to give with servants in your kitchen, a stimulating international environment of people who had actually stepped foot outside their neighbourhood, or fancy dress balls (I actually hate balls so have no idea why I would rhapsodise poetically on them now but you get the picture).

Feeling that you are 'over the hill,' too old to start anything new or have anyone want you for a new project or assignment can be a totally demoralising experience. I have to confess to feeling better when I found out a good friend, an accomplished Danish psychotherapist, spent a year worrying that she would never work again after making a move. Of course she's busier than ever again.

You feel like all those elements which combined to give expatriate life its fairy tale, country club quality have vanished at the stroke of midnight and you are back home carving pumpkins again. Who wouldn't be a bit depressed about this? Add to the mix fruitless career interviews, cleaning your house again for the first time in years, problems with relatives, or a husband stressed out by his job or a commute, and voilà – depression!

It's time to go back to work on your life so you can get to the next stage. I know this for a fact, because after the preceding depressing narrative, I am *officially happy* again as I informed my husband on a day I'm sure he has marked in his calendar as a momentous event. What's more, I know more women like me out there. If you have been struggling through re-entry despair, let me assure you that re-entry shock and all its stages finally, mercifully, ends. But not without some work, so roll up your sleeves and get down to it.

Getting Over It

There comes a day of reckoning when enough is enough! You have two choices here: you can get over it, or you can get over it. No, that's not a typo. Here are some ways, tried and test by myself and others, to help you lift yourself out of that mental and physical exhaustion.

Managing Expectations From Others and Yourself

Expectations overwhelm us without our consent. As I have written, my own expectations about how my life would be after coming home were totally out of whack. I simply expected all sorts of marvellous things to happen to me. When they didn't, my moods fixed themselves to a child's seesaw. Making matters worse than the expectations I heaped on myself, were the expectations outsiders placed on me:

- My husband expected me to be happy now that we were home.
- My kids expected me to be there throughout their adjustment and afterwards too.
- My family expected me to now attend all family functions even though I am a five hour flight from 'home' on the other side of Canada.
- My new community expected up me to start getting into all that life in British Columbia could offer (even though I don't ski) and seemed to be constantly asking me what I had been doing and seeing. It made me feel inadequate.
- Some, not all, new acquaintances I made expected I would 'get over' the previous life and not refer to it anymore because it was outside normal conversation.
- And finally, the expectations I placed on myself to find successful professional situations fuelled by media hype and society's expectation that a paycheque equals some sort of twisted affirmation of your life were likely the most unrealistic of all.

If you recognise yourself in any of those scenarios, put down the whip you have been beating yourself with based on all these unrealistic expectations. That is the first step you must take in order to move on with your life.

Carlanne Herzog suggests here that we should not expect too much of ourselves and that we should try to be with other people, as this usually makes us feel better than being alone. She also suggests that we do not make major life decisions in the middle of a repatriation.

As you move through the mental, emotional and physical transition of repatriation, you must also try not to dwell on negative thoughts. There *will* be a time when you are in balance again.

Find a Good Doctor

Find a good doctor as soon as possible after returning home. If you have a good one at your posting, have a thorough checkup before you leave for home. In North America, finding a new doctor can be difficult as many family practices are filled to capacity and you may need to beg your way into an office. You may also have to shop around before finding someone with whom you are comfortable. When you do find the right doctor, make an appointment to have your hormone levels checked and while you are at it, everything else too. Have a complete overhaul.

Doctors may discover other reasons for what you may perceive as a re-entry gone awry. Certainly this was a case for another middle-aged Canadian woman friend of mine who returned home from the tropics. She suffered from a constant state of a deep freeze, barely able to walk. She thought it was her body's reaction to coming home from a hot climate and mistakenly believed it would fix itself after a few months so she didn't do anything. But finally, after several months of agony, she wrote to me on condition of anonymity, the family knew she had a problem when: "I sat in the car, fully dressed in winter regalia, mittened, hatted, with the heater on full blast, and my husband and daughter were stripped to their waists!"

After worrying it could be arthritis or lupus, a medical diagnosis was finally made: hypothyroidism, which it turns out her own mother had for over twenty years. It's a chronic and common life-long condition which fortunately can be treated with daily medication. So when checking in for a medical overhaul, be sure to have your thyroid function checked too. Many women overlook this. I certainly did. Soon after hearing my friend's story, I went travelling on a speaking tour to Asia, only to return home to sleep so long my husband thought I was in a coma. I immediately went to my doctor. Where I just assumed I was jetlagged and exhausted from talking non-stop for three weeks, it turns out that I too suffer from hypothyroidism.

Be Informed About Menopause and Other Health-Related Issues

Now that you are pulling yourself up from the couch of despair, do not continue to sit in the dark about current health trends. Start reading up on ways to improve the quality of your health, both physical, mental and spiritual. There are so many books on the shelves right now that it may be hard to sift through so much information. So ask your doctor, or seek the advice of a community health worker. Remember you are fresh 'off the boat' and can ask a lot of questions. Ask questions at any time.

Step Back and See Yourself As Others Do

In the midst of the post expat life ennui, it is so important to step back from yourself and start taking steps to create not only your own tailor made reality check, but take the time to place events in their proper perspective. I can say this now looking back, but I certainly (and still do some days) find it difficult to muster the energy all of the time. But I can assure readers that on those days, I remind myself that I am suffering from privileged resentment, that my overseas life had indeed been one of privilege, that I am unbelievably grateful for having had the opportunity to experience all that I did, and that my own personal achievements large or small are worth looking back upon with pride instead of discounting them now that I am home and having a bad day.

To help me keep my perspective, I take lots of walks in a canyon next door to our house. I grab the dog, tramp through the trees and rocks, and remind myself of everything I am grateful for, even little things, like the stream, bits of blue sky through the trees, or the fact that there is no one in sight whom my rambunctious border collie can harass! I feel a lot better after these walks and you will too.

Bring Yourself in From the Margins

I do not believe we are actively marginalised or pushed anywhere by others upon re-entry, even though we feel that often enough to believe it's true. I think we *arrive home on the fringe* and part of the readjustment process is to work our way back into the mainstream.

I personally grew weary of sitting on the outside of my community and was determined not to linger there any longer than need be. Like my American acquaintance on the tennis courts, I desperately need interaction to connect (quite a dichotomy at work for a writer to be sure!) but in order to come in from the sidelines, returnees must figure out a way in.

Think about moving into your own local mainstream through a church or synagogue, maybe the local gym, your kids' school, a local agency that needs volunteers, or if it works for you, a structured job! I started a reading group in my neighbourhood because I had always wanted to, but never managed it abroad. It seemed a great way to meet my neighbours. When potential members protested they were afraid to lead a discussion I said, no problem there! I'll do it! I also got involved with a parent committee for my daughter's band at school. I didn't want to get sucked too deeply into the volunteer vortex before I was ready, so I chose one volunteer committee and stuck to it. And lest I leave anyone with the wrong impression: it took me almost two years to get up the necessary self-confidence and energy to take those small steps. I wish I had done it sooner. By pro-actively bringing myself in from the so-called margins, I felt immediately better. I had taken control of my life.

'Feed Them and They Will Come'

I was lucky enough to speak to a community group in Beijing one spring about the 'joys' of re-entry. After my talk, I was literally embraced by participants who were so happy to hear their needs addressed. (Many of their husbands were busy declaring that going home would be a breeze). A woman whose name I couldn't grab in the blur of well-wishers, nonetheless said something I remember very well and repeat here: "Feed them," she said with great authority, "and they will come."

Her remedy for fighting off feelings of alienation from her community when doing a re-entry, was literally to feed her neighbourhood. She threw open her doors to dinner party after dinner party and in the process met everyone living around her. Likewise, you don't need to make a dinner party to make friends through food: try volunteering at the local food bank and hook up with some other volunteers.

Create Support Groups

If you have trouble regaining perspective by yourself, find others who have shared the experience of living abroad. You can even do that by placing an ad in the local paper. I recently discovered a large restaurant down the road from me used to host an expatriate women's group. Sadly it disbanded because too many members moved! I asked how they found each other and was told they did it through an ad in the paper. So it does work. Many communities have clubs for newcomers.

If no one answers your ad, then seek a professional to talk to about what's on your mind. In short find some way or someone to help you through this phase where you are ready to move on but need a push. As harsh as I may sound handing out this advice, believe me when I say I have been as hard on with myself for moping around feeling sorry for myself just because I couldn't hop on board a 747 and head off to Borneo again. We have enough on our plates just trying to regain our self-image. Self-pity will only drag you further down.

Always a big champion of the support group, I cannot stress enough how important it will be if you truly want to overcome that fatigue and depression to find those pockets of people around you who will understand what it is you are saying when you speak of your expatriate life. And with the magic of internet technology, support groups can be virtual (Check the bibliography for some URLs for expat sites). Your working partner's company may even offer up the names of other returnees if you ask them nicely.

Everyone says that when they return home they want nothing to do with women's clubs, organisations or any other vestiges of the things that suffocated them about expat life. But this may be a case of throwing out the baby with the bath water. Until you have regained your confidence and resettled again, it could very well be that you need to be around (cyberspace is OK too) like-minded people. But they don't magically appear.

When you moved abroad, you made friendship a proactive activity. The same rule applies upon coming home. If you sit back and wait for someone to find you, you may end up doing what I did: lying on a couch all day until it's time to move to the chair you sit in to watch television.

Finally, Quit Blaming Your Partner For Your Depression

How easy it is to assign blame to your partner for all your mood swings. I put my own husband between a rock and a hard place on almost a daily basis. Nothing he could say or do would make me happy because I couldn't get over the feeling that he was responsible for all that I hated about my new life. Conveniently, I blotted out the fact that he was also the reason for most of the good things in my adult life: I had seen a good chunk of the world, met amazing people, and was given the time and freedom to become a full time writer.

That day I could honestly tell him I was *officially happy* was indeed a red-letter day for both of us, not only because I had regained my equilibrium, but because I truly meant it. I still do.

So get up off that couch and get on with your life.

FIVE

WHAT DO YOU WANT TO DO NOW?

PLACING PROFESSIONAL VALUE ON
YOUR OVERSEAS EXPERIENCE

"I am a whole new person now, with much more confidence and I finally have a clear sense of who I was meant to be and where I am going. I am certain this growth would not have come as it did without the experiences gained while abroad."

– posted on the internet by an American woman
on a chat group for expat spouses

Pondering my professional options when I first came home, I scoffed at all suggestions to simply carry on what I had been doing for years, writing and speaking about expatriate life. To anyone who assumed that would seem a logical career choice, my response was automatic and simple: I want to leave my books in a ditch somewhere and just forget I ever wrote them. Everyone within earshot was well aware of the frustrations which had marked my career as an expat author.

Believe it or not, my first book *A Wife's Guide* had been censured by some feminists in the United States when it first appeared in the early '90s. It was at the height of the political correctness ballyhoo. I came under fire for stating what any expat woman knows is obvious: we become dependent when we move overseas. Our portrayal as dependents didn't sit well with some feminists who, at the time, unfortunately for me, were in charge of distribution for a major American book chain. They failed to understand that my book (while cheeky, certainly in the parts I suggested we have babies or manicures to keep body and soul together) offered ways to get over feeling dependent. If only my publisher had stuck to my original title, *A Broad Abroad,* there would have been less confusion over my often irreverent tone.

By the way, those who criticised me had never schlepped an entire family and dog through any Asian airport. Did they really believe that a spouse should be quite capable of landing in a foreign country, immediately finding a new job, and speaking the local language fluently within a week? Dealing with negative, ill-informed reactions from other women, it's easy to understand why the idea of running over my books with a ten ton truck had its appeal.

My career as an expat advocate could at times be equally demoralising. I was burnt out from speaking to human resource directors about family issues and discovering that on the company food chain, we fell somewhere between the furniture and accompanying pets. So when I first came home from overseas, convincing company or government officials to think more about the expatriate family was a war I didn't feel like fighting anymore. Cynical and jaded, I was ready to drop out of my own revolution.

That left me tossing and turning in bed at night, asking myself: *so what do I want to do now?* The women friends I turned to for advice (and not all necessarily expat) shared with me the universal joys of the mid-life professional crisis. They sympathised as I wallowed in middle aged self-pity, lamenting that time had surely passed me by, I was over the hill, used up, and no good to anyone. They too had been there, done that.

Whether legitimate or not, upon returning home I felt I had to *go for it* now, even though I didn't have a clue what *it* might be. I just felt *it* had to be something completely different.

Ignoring the Obvious

Luckily, I was also introduced to people who understood the tight job market and knew better than me the difficulty of an unknown and untested person trying to break into it. These individuals would listen politely as I presented my bona fides and sought advice on what to do next. Bewilderment would cross over their faces as I described the writing niche I had carved out to match my mobile lifestyle. It wasn't that they misunderstood what I had been doing (although we all meet those types who simply don't get anything connected to expat life). They were sincerely baffled by my professional confusion. To them, my options were crystal clear: Build on what you began overseas.

Now that we were home, though, I failed to see any value in continuing what I did abroad. In my mind, writing books about expat life and fighting for family-friendly relocation policies, were just activities I did overseas because I wasn't allowed to do anything else. Why should I do that now that I was home? I dismissed the idea altogether.

It took me two years of heartache, pointless job interviews for positions I knew within seconds would be all wrong for me, and some major and costly missteps (a business partner from hell) to realise my thinking was truly misguided. I steadfastly refused to even contemplate the idea of engaging in work that was connected with my former life even though I had become the writer I always dreamed of being. I thought that walking away from the passion that had fuelled my past and shaped the person I had become, would be as easy as throwing out a moving box or packing case. Worst of all, I mistakenly believed that carrying on with my expat writing and speaking would serve no purpose in building a new life. Boy was I wrong.

Give Credit Where Credit Is Due

When we return home, it is so easy to be blinded by self-pity, exhaustion, rejection, third party scrutiny, and just plain stupidity that we fail to assign any value to the experience we gained as expatriates. In many of our stubborn minds, we believe we are finally home and that must mean the opportunity to have the career we have been postponing for years is within our grasp at last. It just doesn't dawn on us that we have become totally different people, requiring different professional goals and that our overseas experience is a unique asset, not a liability in achieving those new goals.

The moment I realised how much I had changed (not just by enhancing my skill set but also by a major shift in my values system), I could see that my previous life did in fact have merit. But it was up to me to place value on all of the experience I had gained. Once that light bulb went on above my head, I immediately began figuring out a way to re-build my professional life. Among other things, this book got started.

Like magic, once I experienced this valuable epiphany, my whole life started to come together. Direction and purpose began coming into focus. I could finally begin all the community and volunteer activities that had been put on hold until I figured out 'what I was doing.' I felt I could be anything from that point onward because I finally stopped dismissing my past and began appreciating its value to my future.

Work is Personal

Your *life* is your career. Women would better serve themselves by defining the word career as a *path through life*. We should give ourselves permission to customise that path to fit our individual needs, whether it be raising children, looking after ageing parents, travelling, moving for a partner's job, or becoming CEO of a company. Women should try to stop viewing a career as a linear exercise. Throw away ladders and structures and imagine instead a patchwork quilt that illustrates the creative blending of work projects, community and family. But take note that upon re-entry, the quilt, as TCK guru Dave Pollock writes, might need to be turned over to show its plain side to the rest of the world.

The word *career* is a loaded one, able to skewer a woman's self-esteem in a split second. It is a man's word. It implies a certain structure and order and ignores a woman's greatest strength, which is the ability to multi-task. That is, we can have a professional life, a happy marriage and raise healthy children. (However, just because we can do all of those things doesn't mean we have to do them all on the same day. We are not Superwoman). Finally, not to be overlooked is the view society has about the word 'career' – that it supposedly provides a measure of how well life is going, in the form of the weekly paycheque.

It has been gratifying to see that many of the top business gurus in the US, no less than Tom Peters himself, have caught up with my way of thinking.

"It's over. No more vertical. No more ladder. That's
not the way careers work anymore," Peters has written in the techno hip business magazine *Fast Company*. "Linearity is out. A career is now a checker-
board. Or even a maze. It's full of moves that go
sideways, forward, slide on the diagonal, even go
backwards when that makes sense. (It often does). A
career is a portfolio of projects that teach you new
skills, gain you new expertise, develop new capabili-
ties and constantly reinvent you as a brand."

Fast Company (which by the way is a wonderful resource and can be read on line at fastcompany.com)
also has come up with a host of ideas for reinvention,
notably as a *free agent* who can attach themselves to
different projects. The magazine also has finally cot-
toned on to the idea that work is indeed personal and
that while career gurus may disagree on method, they
do share the notion that people do their best when
motivated by a sense of purpose rather than the pur-
suit of money.

I believe expatriate spouses have known all of
these ideas for years as they struggled to have satisfying and full lives abroad. Now we just need to take
the time to remind ourselves of how truly clever we
are when we come home.

The Importance of a Transition Period

A transition period, a time to think and consider
your options, can take place while you are still living
abroad (in the Himalayas for instance with a guru at
your side) or simply during the first six months to
a year after you are back. Regardless of where it occurs, it is wise to set aside a *worry free zone*. This is
a time out to help you avoid the urge to plunge into
the wrong job or situation too soon.

It is important to your mental health to have a transition period (even a short one) to serve as a way station for your mind between what was then and what will be. Sarah Ban Breathnach, whose *Simple Abundance* meditations alternatively irritate me and make me feel grateful for the good fortune that has marked my life, was right on the money about the importance of transition and making changes in your life. "Transformation cannot occur with transition," she writes for May 23rd. As that happens to be my birthday, I took her words as a new age sign.

This transition period does not have to be spent in meditation on a mountaintop nor consumed by a pile of new age spirituality tomes. It could mean working in a shoe store if that makes you happy because it gets you out of the house. The main goal is to have uncomplicated time and space to contemplate what to do next and allow yourself the time to process all that you have experienced and gained while overseas.

Professional Reinvention Also Comes in Three Stages

Re-entry in its broadest sense is a cycle of three stages: closure, chaos and readjustment. Career and life challenges upon repatriation should also be viewed in three important steps.

The first step is clear cut. This is when you bring to closure your expat life and work choices. This can be accomplished by the act of physically moving. Skip to the third step for a moment. This is the stage of readjustment. It is a stage which could be several years down the road. It should be seen as the end result and can only be achieved by taking step number two.

That middle step is the hardest of all. It involves the personal work required for transformation. This work can be any combination of introspection, volunteering, studying, or just experiencing the inevitable hits and misses. This self-development can be accomplished much more easily during a transition period which logic dictates must occur some time between the ending and the beginning of a life change.

Employment Challenges Upon Re-entry

Your overseas experience (and a lot depends on how many years you have lived away and the number and variety of jobs or contracts you have worked at) is often not assigned its true value by potential employers when you first come home. This can and often does lead to frustration and insecurity. Recognise that it is very common to feel that your experience is being viewed as irrelevant. What have you done *here?* you may well be asked.

It simply defies logic, but upon re-entry, you may be turned down for a job not because you are under-qualified, but perversely, because you are over-qualified. Making it worse is that your employment record (six months here, maybe a year there) makes it look like you can't stick to anything. You might as well put the title Flight Risk under your name on those freshly-printed business cards.

But like all the re-entry challenges described in this book, professional challenges can also be met head on and conquered. True, it may seem infuriating in the early days, as my own mother-in-law pointed out to me, to "have all this experience and no place to put it" but eventually you will find the right situation. It won't happen by accident, though. It will require a combination of determination, motivation, introspection and the self-awareness that only you know what will make you happy.

Unhireable But Definitely Employable

For the spouse who has moved home, the word employability will consume table talk and sleepless nights. Finding a way to be considered employable again becomes a holy grail, and the search can sometimes seem as elusive.

The fact is, to a prospective employer who is incapable of thinking outside the box (explanation to follow) our résumés can make us appear to be the exact opposite of employable: unhireable. Given the choice between a résumés of someone who has stayed put for ten years and another who has travelled, the stay-at-home will beat out the flight risk. That's the bad news.

The good news, though, is that in the new work reality, our employability level is actually quite high if we take the necessary action. Career counsellor and author Janis Foord Kirk, whose book *SurvivAbility* (see Bibliography) is tremendously useful when ap plied to mobile women, makes a distinction between employability as action over idea.

"Our employability," writes Foord Kirk, "is our own responsibility. If we keep our skills up to date and actively seek out employers and opportunities, if we professionally give our all to every task we take on, if we're prepared to be creative … we become, in this definition, employable."

Further good news from this career writer is that her idea of survivability in the new work world means flexibility, self-reliance, and the ability to adopt a broader perspective, all qualities which expatriate women have in spades. We just have to make sure we value those qualities in ourselves.

By the way, never overlook the value of volunteer work in enhancing your employability. In the early days before that perfect real job or situation comes along, do not discount the experience and local connections which volunteer work can offer. Nor discount the volunteer work you might have done overseas. Ellen, a Vancouver acquaintance who returned from two postings to South America, found that her old profession (computerised accounting) just wasn't for her anymore. She had spent several satisfying years as a volunteer librarian while abroad and discovered to her amazement and joy, that she wanted to pursue library work once she returned home. She now very happily juggles several part time library positions.

Thinking 'Outside The Box'

When we returned home, I heard the expression "thinking outside the box" repeated more times than I care to remember. As repats, the business reality for us is that our experience lies way beyond the gates of the mainstream because we have lived outside the box. (I'm not talking here about moving boxes).

What exactly is this box? It's really just a comfort zone both social and professional. It's a place from which a potential employer interviews you. It's an emotional area, usually constructed with stable, immovable boundaries, an area which our background in mobility prevents us from penetrating easily upon re-entry. The expat communities we lived in, while certainly capable of being as insular and inward-looking as any small town, nevertheless are painted onto a much broader canvas which provided us with a wider view of the world. At re-entry, we need to meet people who will appreciate that exposure as being valuable to a business or organisation. The search for those like-minded souls can be even more overwhelming than the search for any holy grail.

Many of the people interviewing us cannot picture our box, in the same way friends and family often cannot picture where we have lived. Furthermore, the job interviewer, wanting to play it safe in a time of uncertainty, may not see the value of someone whose thinking is different. Its too scary, for it carries a risk of the unknown and untried. That is just one reality of the new world of work you might come up against.

However, there are people who will find your experience intriguing and worth pursuing for their organisation. They may seem at first to be in a minority and have to be pursued with diligence, but they are out there and you will find them. Your creativity, flexibility, patience, and negotiation and communication skills *will* eventually be appreciated.

And consider looking at your frustrations of being overlooked, ignored, or dismissed this way: When you do connect with the right person or the right company or organisation, your experience is going to make you so much better in the performance of your job than you could possibly imagine.

The New Work Reality

In the new world of commerce, there are no longer jobs for life. People come together as contract teams to work on projects and then disband and move onto new projects. Companies are leaner and meaner than at any time in history. Work is outsourced, allowing a company to pay a consultant or a telecommuter or someone now called an *e-lancer* to do the work an employee used to do, without having to pay the same benefits. Technology has replaced humans and made the humans who can operate technology into worker-bees. The internet and the rise of e-commerce is changing the economic landscape forever.

The nervous, nasty nineties made people meaner. They felt forced to protect their turf or risk being downsized out on the street. This tone will continue to dominate the workplace *zeitgeist* into the new millennium as long as global economies are faltering, prices for natural resources and commodities are fighting their way back up, and downsizing continues to eliminate jobs.

Advances in technology, the kind that were supposed to make our lives easier and not more hectic, will continue to preoccupy people by overwhelming them and fuelling insecurities. In turn, it will make them feel safer by shutting new people out.

It's now a highly competitive jungle out there unless you are returning to previous employers or going back to doing what you did before in institutions like schools or hospitals. Women who believe the time has come to try something altogether new, may find a lot of doors initially closed to them, phone calls and e-mails may go unanswered, and feel that résumés might just as well be thrown into a big gust of wind. Try not to take this personally. People are busier than ever and e-mails, while convenient, can often appear more brusque in tone than was their intention.

I have met people from many walks of life (not just repats) who have had trouble finding a new niche upon moving or when shifting professional gears. They have also sent out hundreds of résumés that went unacknowledged. Knowing this rejection wasn't just happening to me, I stopped personalising it for I realised there was nothing wrong with me.

Patience, planning, unshakeable optimism and our unique experience gained abroad, do pay off eventually. What's necessary is finding a way in, one that can be done without sacrificing or ignoring those valuable assets. So let's get down to it.

Finding Your New Niche

Let me bolster your ego by reminding you of your remarkable ability to find a way into a new world. It may seem trite to say this, and it's certain nobody other than an expatriate spouse would even remotely understand what I'm getting at, but consider all the impossibilities you made possible when you lived abroad. And I don't just mean finding work in a foreign country, toothpicks for a cocktail party, or shoes for your kids. I mean acknowledging the power you don't even know you have which mobility has bestowed upon you, the ability to go with the flow, make a home half way around the world, make new friends, and make a new life altogether. Consider the possibility that you can apply that personal power to figuring out your next move at home. Finding a niche for yourself doesn't begin with the first phone call. It starts with how you feel about yourself before you even pick up the phone.

In the interests of helping at least one woman avoid making some of the mistakes I made, allow me to guide you through some of the emotional sludge which blocked my own head and most definitely slowed my re-entry reinvention almost to a standstill. Later I will offer practical advice too, but I feel that in rising to our professional challenges, we should separate emotional and practical considerations in preparing to look for work. They too can get muddled up. So I will begin with the biggest emotional hurdle of all and that is, knowing when it's the right time to begin looking.

Do NOT Rush Out and Look For Work Immediately

It helps if you feel physically up for the challenge of calling complete strangers out of the blue, introducing yourself, and arranging an initial meeting. So allow yourself the time to decompress and get over the exhaustion caused by the move home first. Then, when you feel better about yourself, it's time to tackle that cold call.

Among other things, when we come home, we have all the wrong clothes for an interview. That Indian cotton blouse, worn with the Mexican skirt and the South American native earrings may look great in a bazaar or at an expat dinner party, but in a corporate boardroom, you will likely resemble some artifact a company executive picked up on a business trip and is now stuck in the corner of the room beside a plastic plant. At least, that's how you will feel about yourself anyway.

By now I expect you've worked out that I never waited until I felt better about myself before trying to plunge into something. I worried about finding work from the moment I stepped off the plane in Vancouver. I always rushed out my door the next day wherever I have moved in the world, my culture shock (in forward gear or in reverse) oozing out of every pore. The inevitable morale-busting disaster always occurred and I ended up feeling about as useful as that ornament stuck on a shelf.

Take the time to catch your breath, get a good hair cut, and buy a simple black pant suit. Then, and only then, can you start your journey into the unknown.

Don't Let Money Matters Make Things Worse (If You Can!)

In that wonderful way of looking at things which husbands are so good at (called hindsight) after two years of being home and watching me spin my wheels and have mood swings that would make a yo yo look like it was standing still, my own wonderful husband did actually say to me one evening: "Maybe it wasn't such a good idea that you looked for work so soon after we got here. Maybe we should have just set some savings aside and given you the time to get back your energy before trying to sell yourself in a new city."

No kidding.

It's true that financial imperatives can drive you out into the workplace. Judging from many women I have spoken to about this, financial issues push them out the door and usually into the wrong job. But stop and think about it for a minute. What's worse? Taking the wrong job right away just to help offset the flying money game? Or avoiding making mistakes by waiting for the right situation to come along when you can make a reasonable decision after your body has had time to recover?

I love my husband's hindsight because it allows me to offer more piece of advice I wish I had taken. If possible (and not everyone has this luxury, I know), set aside funds which can cover the period of time you will definitely need to get your head together. There is a lot swirling around in your head which you should pay heed to before beginning the search for your new life.

Defining Success

What will make you a success? Money? Fame? A flexible work schedule? If you live up to some vague goal stuck in the back of your mind, does that mean you are a success? If you don't live up to it, that is to say you decided to pursue one thing, but accidentally fell into something else which you happened to be good at, will that make you a successful person? Or how about defining the term in the context of the old fashioned and pervasive view that money and success go hand in hand? Will you consider yourself successful only if you make a lot of money? Will you still think you are a success if the price of that top paycheque means never seeing your kids?

The word career is hard enough to define without going crazy. Now add 'success' to the same list of ambiguous words which have a different meaning depending on your point of view. My desk side dictionary, *The New Collins Concise English Dictionary,* apparently shares my values. 'Success' in the first instance is defined as the "favourable outcome of something attempted." 'Success' as defined as the "attainment of wealth and fame" is listed second.

I obviously prefer the first definition, probably because as a writer I would drop dead of a heart attack if I ever made any money. (I have transformed myself from flight risk to impoverished writer according to my husband). That first definition allows me to consider myself successful for attempting to write books and having a favourable outcome to that effort because they are published. If I were to judge myself successful only in terms of wealth and fame, then I am a dismal failure. I don't believe that for a second. All right, maybe on a cold, rainy day when the computer screen remains blank in front of me I don't feel so successful.

When reinventing yourself upon re-entry, defining success will be an important exercise. It will help you identify your challenges and set goals. It is an exercise in examining your own values system. What you believe to be important in life, home, children, husband, extended family, community, church, just making a difference to an individual or a community, will impact on the decisions you will now take to shape your new life at home. Try not to allow yourself, in the early days for sure, to be suckered into believing that only money equals success. You could be setting yourself up for failure before you even begin your search. Keep in mind that all forms of success carry some kind of price. What are you willing to pay?

Work and Family Balance

In the real world of home, balancing work and family is an on-going battle for women, a battle you may not have been waging for a few years while abroad. Even those of us privileged enough to have a choice to stay home are not exempt. We also fight the emotional imbalance created (sometimes by financial imperatives, more often by the need to work for the sake of our identity) by the urge to nurture over the urge to make the money which society, in the end, will use as a measuring stick.

The operative word here, I believe, is *balance*.

When we returned home and my husband's new job had him on the road half the time, I had to be the parent sticking close to home. This obviously was a major factor impacting on my employment choices. Despite my idea that I was coming home to finally pursue a career, I quickly realised, just who was I kidding? If I took a full time job, I would be so off balance by the burden of my responsibilities I would be walking at a ninety degree angle.

You will hear from those around you (people who have not moved around) that your children will be OK if you immediately sign on for a full time job because there are lots of single working parents around and they cope don't they? Do not let that confuse our own issues. Those kids of single parents (and yes they have tremendous issues to deal with too) nonetheless do not have your children's issues of having been uprooted from country to country.

I have always stressed that in order for mobile wives to be happy, we need to stick to our own gut feelings on issues and not be swayed by what others think we should be doing. If your children still need you around, especially in the early days of your return, than all of your work plans will have to factor in their presence. It could be that someone will offer you the job of the century during this period, but if it requires 50-60 hours a week of your time, with road trips to Cleveland while your partner is also travelling, just who is going to be looking after the children during this time?

Looking for Work at a 'Certain Age'

Earlier, I raised the connection between menopause and re-entry shock. It does take on another twist, though, if you are desperately seeking employment or a change in your career at the same time as the biggest physical change in your life (or in the years leading up to it). If you are still ambitious enough to want to get back into your career, or find a new one, it's wise to know in advance that the convergence of the mood swings associated with perimenopausal and menopausal hormonal changes to your body and the ups and downs caused by the emotional beating to your self-esteem by looking for work can not only get you down, but can literally knock you out cold.

As I said earlier, I have joked when addressing expatriate audiences of women about not coming home until after menopause and it is usually in connection with finding a new professional niche. When the laughter subsides (for a topic no one wants to talk about, it is amazing how I seem to be virtually guaranteed a giddy response), I try to point out that some menopausal symptoms can make a woman over-react and overly-sensitive. Feelings of rejection which may come in a job search can definitely be heightened by hormones.

Expectations Can Kill Motivation

If there was one single biggest expectation that killed me about trying to have a career at home, it was just that: believing that after fifteen years of moving around, I expected I could *easily* have a career at home. My thinking was absolute. My expectations seemed perfectly normal to me. In my view, all that was required was that I stay put for a while and I would be find something creative and satisfying to do.

I confused the words *expectation* and *entitlement*. Why else would I believe so strongly that after having the unbelievable good fortune of leading an expat life, travelling hither and yonder, having wonderful help when my children were young and so on that I would not carry on with this fairy tale life and live happily ever after in the work world of Canada?

Never abandon your hopes and dreams. Without them you might as well roll over and die. Hope keeps us motivated. It certainly helps swing the mood to the up side. But like going abroad, where I recommended motivation, self-discipline, and the ability to get out there and create it yourself because nobody is going to do it for you, turn the scenario around and apply it when you get home. Just because you are back to stay does not mean you should expect to automatically find something to do or that your telephone will ring off the hook. If that doesn't happen immediately, you have to remain motivated. You also have to remain positive. And if you have rested up, experienced a transition period, and shed the crazed maniac look and exotic accessories (at least for interviews), it's a lot easier to get yourself in gear.

It's OK To Be Scared

Fear is one final emotion worth mentioning for the role it plays in the challenging search for meaningful employment when you come home. It may be fear of rejection or perversely, fear of acceptance (and then fear of not being able to perform a job you have talked your way into). There is not a person alive who hasn't felt nervous when embarking upon an unknown situation. But as author Barbara Sher points out in her bestselling career bible *Wishcraft: How to Get What You Really Want:* "There's nothing in the world that's worth doing that isn't going to scare you."

To her readers looking to make changes in their professional lives, Sher writes: "What you really are is scared. You're probably embarrassed to admit it, even to yourself, because you are a grown up and you're not supposed to be afraid of anything. But there are a few thousand reasons to be scared when you start going for what you want."

My own biggest fear during my professional re-invention? "Maybe I have vastly over-rated myself," I would quietly mutter to my husband after yet another professional misadventure in my early days of repatriation. "Don't be ridiculous," was his response. Even though his words were not quite the comfort I was seeking, I did listen to him from time to time.

This Doesn't Happen to Everyone

I will continue to stress that not everyone will experience career re-entry problems. For those people born under the big magic white light which perpetually shines extraordinary good luck down upon them, chances are a career is waiting for them at the arrival desk at the airport. But in the real world, ordinary mortals must make their own luck. And remember this is the same real world where time has marched on while we have been away, where computers have become so complex that only our children can figure out how to work them, and (if you re-entering in your forties) where ageism is a prevailing workplace attitude. Try to see career challenges in this real context rather than one we might only wish for, or worse, expect. And if none of this applies, consider yourself lucky and help someone else.

Some Practicalities of Looking for Work

Now that many of the emotional challenges have been touched upon, some more irreverently than others, you must now learn to remove emotion from your job search. As my husband has told me over and over again, I should not allow emotion to be a factor in business. Of course I will be able to live up to that advice on the same day the sun comes up blue and my curly hair goes straight. Until that day, consider some practical tips I learned from my own experience and from others:

Engage a Career Counsellor or Mentor

This could be the easiest phone call you make, to a qualified, professional career counsellor whose job it is to help you sort through and make sense of your extensive round the world employment history. Try to get your husband's company to pay for career counselling sessions upon re-entry to determine what you know how to do. Many companies will pay for this service for the spouse, so find out if your husband's company is one of them. If the company hasn't done so in the past, that doesn't mean it won't begin now, with you. Asking for what you need upon re-entry is a good first step in entering into the strange and often foreign corporate culture. I wish I had used such a service not only to help me write a new résumé, but also plough through my existing one and identify my skills worth selling. If you can't engage a counsellor, try reading *A Career in Your Suitcase* by Joanna Parfitt (see Bibliography) for its sound advice on helping you identify skills and strengths which will apply on re-entry as much as going overseas. Find a mentor, someone in your field or just a good, common sense person with a lot of ideas and connections.

Find Your Focus

Until you know what you want to do, you will never know what you are selling. Write that down somewhere and stick it where you can always see it. Focus is an essential ingredient for success, however you define it.

How will you know what you want to do? Unless you have traditional job skills such as administrative, teaching, or health care related, you will have spent the transition period thinking long and hard about who you want to be. Now you must act on it.

Deciding on a path to take will not only work miracles on the state of mental health, but you will be amazed at how much knowing what you want to do will help you market yourself when the right time arrives. Without focus, you risk going out to prospective employers sounding confused and dazed.

A word of caution: sometimes your focus can be blurred by the overwhelming advice from well-meaning friends, family, or new contacts who always begin a sentence with: you know what you should do? They then go on and on about options you have either considered and dismissed; options the person advising you would never dream of doing in a million years; or describe a job you had twenty years ago. Be ready to face some frustrating days and try not to lose your friends. Nod and say you will consider their advice and get back to them. Sometimes, however, it does take an outsider to be objective about your real strengths. Some of your friends may talk sense.

Write Your Own Mission Statement

If the question 'And what do you want to do now?' makes you want to fling yourself off the nearest cliff, then you need a ready answer to that question to stop you from jumping. One way to develop that answer (and coincidentally help sharpen your focus too) is to write your own mission statement. It doesn't need to be long, in fact two sentences will do. Even just five words will work. *I write books for expatriates.* That's mine, but it took me over two years upon my own re-entry to see that.

A mission statement is not a static object. Once developed and written, it shouldn't sit in a file or drawer and never looked at again. It needs to be nurtured and constantly re-examined. Mission statements not only need to be re-visited on a regular basis, you need to work on your mission statement. In the case of a repatriated spouse, this means that you must be ready to expend a tremendous amount of creative energy to make that mission statement come true.

There are many ways to develop your mission statement. Helen Eriksen, a Danish executive coach, gave a workshop entitled "Writing Your Own Mission Statement" at the most exciting women's conference I have ever had the good fortune to speak at: *Working Internationally Now* (WIN) held every year in Milan. (check out www.winconference.com for details).

Rather than attack the mission statement using our skills inventory which many of us often do, Helen asks participants to focus on what I can only paraphrase as a *values inventory*. She suggests this route because she believes a mission statement must begin with a person's core values. I endorse this idea because we come home with not only a different skill set, but let's face it, our values have also changed profoundly as a result of our experience.

In one of many intriguing exercises, Helen asks participants to make a list of their successes and match them with what they believed was the core value (that can be an attitude or characteristic as much as a belief) which contributed to the success. Part of my own list, to give you an idea of how it worked, went like this: Success? My books. The values driving that success? My humour and honesty. Another success? Managing to be available as much as possible to my children. My core value? The importance of pro-active parenting. Get the picture? Suddenly you can see in black and white that more than the ability to do something like write or speak or count or analyse may be key indicators in your search for what you want to do next with your life.

Carlanne Herzog also endorses the value of writing a mission statement, but would also like us to remember our general and specific knowledge skills. Innate general skills such as organisational, linguistic, writing or verbal are valuable in a variety of work situations. Specific knowledge skills may need to be updated, but don't forget to give yourself credit for them.

Marketing Materials

More practically, now that you are now about to promote "Brand You" as the business magazines will call you, as a very first step, a business card should be printed up as well as an up to date résumé. Depending on what you are selling, a career portfolio could also be put together (explanation to follow). Some business cards now even have a mission statement written on the back.

In this age of the internet, do not immediately dismiss the idea of putting together a web site, initially to promote what you do and later, to engage in e-commerce. When we first returned, my older brother kept asking me why I didn't put together a web site immediately. I told him I was having enough trouble figuring out e-mail at that time.

Marketing yourself, especially at the beginning, should be seen as a full time job. Be sure you have the proper materials with which to do so.

Career Portfolios

Instead of just handing someone a xeroxed copy of your résumé, consider the career portfolio as a way of introducing your work to a prospective employer. It's not just artists and designers anymore who use a portfolio to market their talents.

In his book *Portfolio Power,* author Martin Kimeldorf believes portfolios are for artefacts, not facts, and can be made up of certificates, references, samples of your work, thank you notes, employee evaluations, statistics or newspaper clippings as just a few examples. Kimeldorf suggests you compile all these pieces of your professional history using clear A4 wallets inside a ring binder, categorising sections using headings such as Learning, Communication and Persuasion Abilities, Managerial or Leadership Skills, and Information Gathering. Try to limit the portfolio to 20 items if possible.

Take this portfolio with you along on all interviews, whether they be informational or for actual interview situations. Use the portfolio during your meeting as a way of introducing yourself and your work. Prepare a bit of a set piece story about specific items that will show you off in the best light without over-doing it. Think of some of the pieces of the portfolio as your cue cards to explain your working life. If you feel you cannot afford to leave the entire portfolio behind each and every time, then have at hand several extra copies of some of its key pieces that you can attach to your résumé.

Re-educate Yourself for a Career Shift

During the transition period, many women have found that going back to school to take courses that either pique their interest or to retrain for something new altogether works well during the process of their professional reinvention. Lise, a Canadian acquaintance and former foreign service wife, retrained (by correspondence) to enter the investment world and now happily works as a stock broker. Other women have told me that just signing up for a language course helps get their brain back in gear as well as providing some structure to their day. Regardless of your motives, in your down time while you are considering your options, do check out local educational institutions to see if there may be a course which can provide you entry into a new industry. And don't overlook studying by correspondence or over the internet.

Networking

The more people you talk to, the more people you can learn from, and who may be able learn from you. Donna Messer, a Canadian networking guru who speaks internationally about networking, maintains that the most effective networking happens when you give as well as take. Join local women's groups, business groups, or support groups of any kind as a way of researching the job market. Find out how things work and who some of the key local players may be in your city or town.

For those of us who hate live functions where you may feel awkward or out of place (people find it odd, but I hate promoting myself in front of real, breathing people), the internet has been a godsend. Connect via the internet through chat groups and on line support groups. It's amazing what can be accomplished using what I call *cyber chutzpah*. That's my own brazen method of sending out e-mails to people I don't know to see if they would be interested in having me come to speak. Cyber-networking is much easier than a phone call because you actually write out what you want to say instead of stumbling over your words in a complete panic when you actually reach a live voice on the telephone.

Consider Self-Employment

Women represent a high percentage of self-employed entrepreneurs. It may be that a home-based business appeals to mothers still at home with kids or who want to be available for driving duties. Regardless of the motivation, there has never been a better time, once again thanks to the internet, to start your own business. Become a Dot Com business by setting up a web-based business. Or consider a consultancy of any kind (remember all that international experience you have?) and promote yourself via the internet. There are a thousand and one business ideas out there. If you have one, and the idea of working for yourself and setting your own pace and hours appeals to you, just pick up any business magazine and you will find a section devoted to entrepreneurship and small business. Consult your local bank for small business loans. And then get busy writing a business plan.

Live Local/Work Global

If you do go into business for yourself, it may be that your market is global rather than local. Considering the international experience you have returned home with, this is not an idea too far outside the realm of possibility.

In a nutshell, this idea means you export your expertise and import money. Or so you would hope. Obviously, the age and stage of your children will impact on this option if travel is involved, but the internet once again has opened up the possibilities of selling your services to companies that may not be in your own neighbourhood. In the new world of work, the e-lancer is becoming more commonplace. It might work for you.

Avoiding HUGE Mistakes

When we move home, we want our life in order immediately and in our haste and fragile vulnerable states we can make mistakes that are costly both financially and emotionally. I fell victim to both. Living overseas, I dreamed of having my own communications company. It was always a pipe dream when we were moving around. What was the point of starting a company that needed a home base? Too soon after re-entry I found myself in a business partnership for a communications company. Had I sat down and analysed my former partner and whether or not I personally would fit into a partnership situation, I would have stopped the idea before it began. My marriage partnership is about all I can handle.

It seems that re-entry can cause a lot of false professional starts for many repatriated women who find themselves looking everywhere for new opportunities. We run around chasing both our tails and our fate, wondering which way to go or try in vain to find a crystal ball with a clear picture of our destiny. Accept the idea that the first thing you do may be just the first of many projects which won't necessarily last forever. Given the changing nature of work itself, it might just be that you will go from one project to another for the rest of your life. And that's OK too.

Professional re-entry isn't like rearranging the furniture in your house. It won't be a static process. Like your mission statement, it will need to be worked on, finessed, and altered. Some patches of your quilt may have lost their lustre.

One Final Pep Talk About Motivation

Like my swami advised me, surround yourself with positive, upbeat people and I guarantee their optimism will rub off. Give yourself a swearing box and deposit money every time you think a negative thought. Monitor your progress diligently. Make a commitment to yourself. That could be as simple as joining a network of some kind or assigning yourself one personal management task each week. "Proactive people take their weather with them," says Kit, a good American friend and wise counsellor who has seen her share of the world with her military husband (and helped a lot of women in the process).

We so often tie up our self-image and self-worth with what it is we are doing for a living. Take away employment, and self-esteem (the way we look at ourselves and assign value) plummets. That's because we have come to believe our identity relies on what we do rather than who we are. We feel there is no possible way to change this situation overnight. Or is there? Existential or essential? Only you know best which matters most to you.

I believe that so much of what we allow to bother us about this situation is in our heads. We allow thoughts to provoke our emotions and send us into tailspins.

Since I am as guilty of this as the next woman, I find it hard to write too many helpful ways to avoid those negative thoughts which won't sound empty. I freely admit I ignored much of the sound advice which came my way. But Carlanne Herzog reminds us that negative self-talk causes our body to tense and become stressed, which in turn can lead to more anxiety, anger, guilt and a greater sense of worthlessness.

My own professional re-entry was obviously miserable when it clearly didn't need to be. But in order to keep my self-esteem healthy, I did force myself to remain motivated. It was only when I was in motion that I felt optimistic that something would finally break my way.

I also put my sense of humour in a stranglehold so I wouldn't lose it. I took every opening available to make myself laugh rather than cry. When I ran away from the airport in that horrible debacle I described earlier, I laughed out loud in my car as I debated a mundane decision over where I would stop to buy chicken I needed for dinner that night. I even worked out a wonderful voice mail message to leave with people who couldn't be bothered to call me back: "I'm doing a story about people who don't call back and need to talk to you about it."

Amazing how that strategy worked. Not only did it make people call me back, but more importantly, helped me feel a lot brighter about the professional possibilities that awaited me in my future. All those possibilities are out there. It's now up to you to find them. You can do it.

SIX

RE-ENTRY RAGE AND RESENTMENT

GETTING OVER IT

"I wanted to pursue some self-development activities once we were home, but my spouse accused me of being selfish. I was angry, especially as it was coming from a man who now had nothing to do all day."
— Forty-something Australian woman whose partner left the corporate world.

Much of our first year at home is a blur in my mind. I haven't blotted it out entirely though, because I can still recall and hang my head in shame at the memory of the juvenile temper tantrums I threw. Fortunately, my fits occurred mostly when I was alone. One particular four letter word seemed to emerge with frightening regularity, usually delivered at the top of my lungs and too often directed at our puppy who was a convenient target for my wrath. The intensity of my tantrum would depend on what household item our energetic young pet had destroyed that day (my prescription sunglasses, my daughter's bed, a chunk of a wall in the front hall, or a precious Indian carpet I hand carried from New Delhi). On other days, I displayed the amazing dexterity required to rant and drive at the same time, usually while ferrying my daughter to school for an early morning band rehearsal.

During those crack of dawn venting sessions in the car, my message to my daughter was always the same: grow up and be a man, I would tell her, for clearly the world was created to accommodate men and leave women to look after all the details. Fortunately, Lilly has always been more mature than her mother. She would allow me to blow off steam about the so-called injustice, as I saw it, of being relocated into a great new house, in one of the most beautiful cities in the world, enjoying one of the highest qualities of life.

Sadly, it is the human condition to feel dissatisfied even when life couldn't be more pleasant. I felt my rosy new picture wasn't complete because my partner was gone most of the time and I was failing so miserably to find meaningful employment. In retrospect (and after my husband read this manuscript and made wonderful notations like, *that might have been your view of things* in certain sections) I know I was being incredibly unfair to him. But at the time, who wanted to be fair?

My daughter still remembers our mutual hysteria early after our move home when a brand new dishwasher exploded and we stepped into several feet of hot water gushing everywhere. Her father was out of town, beginning a pattern of convenient absence. We couldn't see into the future to know that this would always be so: whether it was bad plumbing karma or a family crisis, we could safely be assured that he would be on the other side of the world leaving us to mop up. The dishwasher debacle was only the beginning of a series of crises on the home front when one partner (the same one) always seemed to be away. There were mice infestations, two extraordinary basement floods within weeks of each other proving that lightening can strike in the same place twice, and probably the worst where-is-my-husband-when-I-need-him scenario of all: a man banging on our front door in the middle of the night asking to use our phone because his hand was bloody and he would "give me twenty bucks if I opened the door!" Baseball bat in one hand, and telephone in the other, it was a toss-up as to who I was going to call: 911 for assistance, or my husband to scream at him. I chose the police. In my universe at that time, I truly felt they were more reliable.

What (or Who) Are We Angry At?

Since I need to keep this book shorter than *War and Peace*, I can't identify everything that makes our blood boil when we return, but anger and resentment are clearly two major emotions driving mood swings and/or depression. And sometimes, when we're just not sure what we are so angry about, there sit our partners (if they are in town) as convenient targets. Everything has to be their fault, right? Not really. But it's easier to blame our partners than to examine our own personal contributions to re-entry rage. Believe it or not, I will not be blaming every one of my mood swings on my partner.

Interestingly, Carlanne Herzog tells us that anger is almost always fear in disguise, and that we are often not really upset for the reason we think. Being aware of your anger is often the first step to moving through it.

Some spouses are angry at family and friends who don't or won't understand their shock; at companies which don't facilitate a smoother welcome home; or just at themselves for not coping better with their situations. I will get to all of these themes as this chapter unfolds.

The Following May Be Politically Incorrect

At the risk of being chastised yet again for being politically incorrect for writing about issues unique to female and not necessarily male spouses, allow me to qualify the comments to follow in this chapter.

Male spouses who move for their wife's job may, in fact, feel the same way as a female spouse. I firmly believe, however, that most men handle the same issues in a different way. I doubt, for instance, that my husband would have been angry at me if I wasn't home the night the dishwasher exploded. He just wouldn't have felt as *helpless* as I did. (Feminists may go ahead and shudder at the word helpless but I can't sugar coat my own ineptitude except to say I now know how to shut the water off).

Men also do not define or measure themselves the same the way women do. They won't cancel plans in a fit of rage because they feel too bloated to put on the clothes selected for the days outing. Unlike women, men don't watch their moods, self-esteem, self-image, and confidence go from highs to lows so many times in one day that they can completely forget by days end, if it had been a good day or a bad one.

Privileged Anger and Resentment

One more qualifier is necessary to a discussion about anger. At the risk of repeating myself, I do need to state again that it is indeed a privilege to move around, experience the world, give our children a global view and all the other wonderful fringe benefits associated with life as an expat. Likewise, coming home, with our memories, our global experiences, our photo albums, our home movies, our *foreign stuff* are even more reasons to feel lucky. When

I write about anger and resentment, it is with the understanding that the greater context for this discussion acknowledges that gratitude.

However, to *deny* that we are angry and resentful is unhealthy. These emotions can create tension in our lives and our marriages, especially if they go unarticulated.

When I raised the subject of my own fifteen years of pent up anger and resentment with my partner, he replied with his usual touch of irony: "You mean you kept it pent up?"

When Does the Anger Surface?

Anger and resentment usually coincide with the end of the honeymoon period. This shouldn't surprise anyone who has experienced the same emotions abroad, for they appear overseas at roughly the same point in the culture shock cycle. The thrill of the new place is wearing off and reality sets in. When you return home, and that reality is not anything like you expected it to be, you get mad. And who better to get mad at than your partner?

When combined with those of us having mood swings, the impact of re-entry rage on our marriages should be obvious. We aren't easy to live with when we are suffering re-entry shock. We tend to save the up times for strangers and let our hair down, literally, with our mates. They, more than any other person in our lives, see the dark and depressed side of our lives. And that can put a very heavy strain on a marriage.

What Causes Our Anger?

In her bestselling book *The Dance of Anger,* author Harriet Lerner examines anger and its role in intimate relationships. Dr. Lerner writes about the process of de-selfing which happens when "one person, often a wife, does more giving in and going along than is her share and does not have a sense of clarity about her decisions and control over her choices." Sound familiar?

"The partner who is doing the most sacrificing of self stores up the most repressed anger and is especially vulnerable to becoming depressed and developing other emotional problems," writes Dr. Lerner noting that a woman "may express her anger at inappropriate times, over petty issues, in a manner that may invite others simply to ignore her or to view her as irrational or sick."

A loss of self can also lead to feelings of emptiness, according to Dr. Kirsten Thogersen, an expatriate Danish psychotherapist who has counselled international families and in particular, expat spouses for almost twenty years.

"Women's goals and perspectives are social," Dr. Thogersen wrote to me during the research of this book. "Ask most women about their dreams in life, and they will provide answers which have something to do with love, social commitment, the people around them, art, expression, growth and development. Women find themselves in their exchanges with friends, children, family, school and nature. Once we lose all of those elements during an international move, we lose ourselves."

However, unlike losing a loved one who can be mourned and cried over before you eventually reach a point of healing, Dr. Thogersen believes that when we lose ourselves, we don't feel the same sadness. We feel empty.

"That emptiness can turn into feelings of anger. We move from one emotion to the other, often within hours of the same day," she believes. "And the anger one feels when empty and lost has a desperation to it. It is different from the good, creative anger we need to lead a healthy life. This desperate anger is deep and horrible and yet we can trick ourselves into making it sound like natural anger. It isn't, and professional help is often required to separate the healthy anger from the desperate and destructive anger and anxiety stemming from the loss of self during a moving crisis."

It is only by understanding the core of the anger, Dr. Thogersen believes, that women can be more assertive in the process of finding situations which make them feel like themselves again.

There are specific triggers unique to repatriation which will also cause anger to surface. Keep in mind that I am only identifying some areas that set women off into that horrible state of over-reaction to situations which, if they were not exaggerated by the move home, would likely never bother us. Or certainly bother us less.

Unfulfilled Professional Expectations

Unfulfilled expectations can frustrate, demoralise and ultimately enrage any individual from the age of two onward. A mature woman who is feeling exhausted from a move, settling children in new schools or universities, or getting used to cleaning her oven again after years of household help, can't possibly be immune to feeling just a bit out of sorts over this whole re-entry experience.

Women who expected to come home and establish a new professional identity or career, tend to personalise what can be a prolonged waiting period required to re-establish themselves. By that I mean rejection hits harder and closer to home than it should. As I noted in the previous chapter, far from finding satisfying work right away, many women discover their résumés, which emphasises skills and experience over stable employment records, have made them virtually unemployable. Who wouldn't be angry when skills go unrecognised or under-utilised?

Pressure to find Work

There is an old story that husbands and wives fight mostly about sex and money and it definitely holds true in the latter case for many returning couples. Lucky are those who repatriate without financial worries. Some women end up taking jobs they don't want because the financial wolf is howling at the door and this doesn't create a happy situation. Financial pressures and a returning spouse's desire to find satisfying work after years abroad, can often be a deadly combination which ends up in not only serious arguments, but tremendous feelings of anger.

Some repatriated spouses suddenly have to find gainful employment to pay the mortgage or to keep the family in the style to which they grew accustomed abroad. When employment isn't easily available, it can put a lot of pressure and strain on the family. Enter another favourite emotion: guilt. Women may feel they aren't pulling their weight financially, yet are unable to do so because no one will hire them. This conundrum presents a common impasse.

Responsibilities on the Home Front

When it seems only you are adjusting to the fact that there is no longer household help or overseas allowances to help cushion your re-entry, the target of your anger (the one who lives on Mars while you live on

Venus) usually doesn't get it. It's like two people looking at the same picture and seeing entirely different
views and one of them still sees a maid or driver in
it who looks remarkably like you. It seems you will
never agree on anything, unless it is to see a marriage
counsellor, a choice many couples must ultimately
make (if they can afford it).

There is a terrible irony at work again: women
who felt a profound loss of independence when they
first agreed to move abroad with their partners, always felt in the back of their minds that they would
reclaim that independence when they returned home.
Things don't always turn out that way. When work
neither magically nor easily appears, a repatriated
wife may slowly realise that she may now be just as
dependent on her husband as before, only without
the excuse of living in a foreign country. That's a
scary thought. Dependence and fear can also breed
anger and resentment.

Anger at the Company

There can be many reasons why a repatriated spouse
is angry at the people who sent her family overseas in
the first place beginning with the worst case scenario:
the working partner is downsized out of a job and
unceremoniously returned to home base with no employment prospects, often in the middle of a school
term. After that, anger will emerge depending on individual situations.

If the working partner is repatriated to headquarters, only to find that there is no interesting job to
go to, much of the employee's frustration will come
home at the end of the day and be dumped onto the
dinner table.

The most infuriating situation for the accompanying spouse is to learn that the company, organisation, government, or whoever sent the family abroad, will be doing nothing for the family to ease the transition of re-entry of coming home. When a spouse hears once again that 'You're home now, so what's the problem?' either from the company directly or through its mouthpiece (her partner) blood pressure can begin to rise, especially if she hears how more enlightened companies are now engaging in re-entry training and support.

Kathy, an American repatriated spouse, wrote to me about her anger in what she admits now was not her finest moment, "I was unreasonably angry at my husband. At one point, I yelled at him, in front of our son that I hated him over and over again. It was horrible! And I will never forgive (her husband's employer) for our treatment. There was no compassion or help or understanding from anyone! They have no idea or care to know what they put us through." Kathy is quick to add that "as a family we are in a much better place now" but like many of us, she has tried to blot those early angry days from her memory banks. It's painful to remember ourselves as some other person altogether.

When the Working Spouse Continues to Travel

During the course of our fifteen years in the foreign service, my partner travelled several times a year, typically for two or three week stretches, leaving me behind to cope with our young children, my own work, and if we were living in Canada at the time, usually a snow or ice storm of the century. When we moved to Vancouver, I thought that at last we would all stay put. Who was I kidding? He had taken a job to mar-

ket Canadian education in the international marketplace. Did I think that marketplace was down our
suburban road and not across oceans and continents?
I never really thought it all through. I would have
been a lot better off if I had.

Business people on the road all the time are known
as *road warriors*. Those of us who married these
warriors certainly know how to make war, usually
the minute they finally walk in the door after their
third trip that month. That's if you haven't had a
full blown fight over the phone. My anger over my
partner's incessant travel took the form of a missile
I took every opportunity to shoot straight through
his heart. Like so many others, I had to cope with re-
entry shock virtually alone.

Friends and Family Don't Get It Either

Sometimes, friends and family also don't understand,
quite literally, where you are coming from. Many
want you to stop talking about the time you went
here or there or bought this or that. You are home
now and raising subjects like re-entry shock (and
watching your friends eyes roll) makes you feel both
alien and alienated. In that isolation, you stew in
your own juices.

Overseas, you often couldn't communicate with
local people and that frustration contributed to culture shock. Upon returning home, the same frustration of trying to explain to people why one day they
may see you wearing a smile and the next day a terrible, stressful looking grimace, may also fall on deaf
ears and this too can make you angry. No one is feeling sorry that you are struggling to clean windows
for the first time in years. One too many friends tell
you to be patient about settling in as they sit in the

comfort of their beautifully renovated home in which they have lived for twenty years, or to calm down about finding satisfying work as they head off to their corporate jobs or work away at lucrative contracts. Meanwhile, you just want to scream in frustration.

Worse, we tend to be terribly judgmental when we come home, another irony considering we have supposedly raised our levels of tolerance living abroad. Anger is only one step removed. Why don't people see how great they have it? How many times have you wanted to shout that from a roof top?

Feeling Like an Outsider

Returning home, especially to communities where a newcomer is sighted every decade or so, makes many women feel out of the social loop. It's hard to make new friends these days, harder still at a later age when your children no longer provide the automatic entrée they once did. In Vancouver, we quickly learned that you met more people walking your dog than over a coffee in the neighbourhood coffee house unless you brought your dog with you, in which case, conversation about pets flows.

My children can't get over the fact that when I was growing up, I knew the name of every family on our street. At re-entry, the lack of connection with neighbours and community which is prevalent in society can initially make you feel exhausted (as explored in Chapter Four) and then sad and lonely: emotions which can turn quickly into anger. Why doesn't anyone invite new people over anymore? In the new high tech world, many people don't have the time or interest for making new friends in the neighbourhood. And just when you finally have a coffee or dinner date lined up, you become victim of the latest social malaise: the last minute cancellation.

Is This All There Is?

The notion that the interesting part of your life has now ended can also contribute to anger and resentment. These feelings can be heightened if your partner is continuing to lead an interesting life while you walk the dog and take out the garbage. During the re-entry period, and especially during the post-honeymoon crash, the feeling that nothing exciting could possibly happen to you again after a life abroad where you never knew what could happen next can at first depress and later anger you. It's hard to focus on the new challenges and turn them into opportunities (which you will do eventually), just as you did while living overseas. It's harder, of course, because there are fewer people around to empathise or support you but remember that only makes success when it does come all the more sweeter.

'Rage Against the Ordinary'

American author Barbara Sher, whose book *Wishcraft* on career and life development I discussed in Chapter Five, offers some extremely thought-provoking insights on the subject of rage in her 1994 bestseller *I Could Do Anything If I Only Knew What It Was*. Sher writes about 'rage against the ordinary.'

Sher believes that many career seekers set their sights way too high and their attitudes end up foiling their ability to find meaningful work.

"If you're in a rage against the ordinary, you don't want to be a painter, you want to be the greatest painter. ... Glory is so important to you that you're impatient with the chores and details that make life work. ... You deserve a big hit and you want it now. You don't have the time or inclination to build the foundation of skills and know-how that would actually get you a hit," she writes. Ragers, according to Sher, believe they are special people and therefore should not have to do anything but what they truly want to do or their specialness will vanish.

Many returning expats (children as well as adults) have noted that upon returning from living abroad, they feel they no longer are special, either to their family who found them alternatively exotic and tedious for living the overseas life or to the community at large, including potential employers. Without the expat badge to identify themselves, they revert to ordinary folk, the kind who work 9–5 to pay off mortgages and mow the lawn on the weekends.

Looking back on the early days of my own re-entry (and the way I approached finding work and new friends), I immediately could identify with Sher's observations about rage. For instance, given my overseas qualifications, especially in the Asia Pacific region with which Vancouver is tightly connected, I mistakenly believed that employers should have been clamouring for my services. When they didn't, I was angry at what I perceived as narrow minded, parochial thinking. I certainly didn't want to take any job that I felt was beneath my level of experience. I was, in fact, raging against the ordinary mortal I had become in my new community. So I had to change the way I looked at things. I had to accept the hard truth that being in a new town, I had go back to the bottom of the heap and start working upward again.

Further exasperating situations like mine and that of other women, was the feeling that after following my husband's career for so many years, I now deserved a professional break. This sense of entitlement is also addressed by Sher in her explanation of rage against the ordinary. Sher links this notion of passively waiting to be discovered to a righting of past wrongs in life. She uses case studies and personal stories of people who believe that if something traumatic happened to them in their childhood (death, abandonment, or abuse by a parent are just a few examples she cites), by the time they reach adulthood, they have an overwhelming desire to settle old scores and feel only some earth shattering career break will right past wrongs.

Mulling over these passages, and recognising that Sher did not have expat audiences specifically in mind when she wrote her book, I nevertheless clearly saw a link between my rage at my husband (for trotting off to another exciting career challenge) and my own frustration at not finding something fantastic for myself within weeks of our return home. I felt like most expats do (but couldn't articulate it at the time) that I was special, that I had been wronged somehow (following my partner), and now it was *my* turn. Nothing less than an extraordinary employment opportunity was owed to me.

Wrong again! It took me several years of disillusionment, frustration, and ultimately hitting rock bottom in my new workplace to get over this misguided sense of immediate entitlement. It would seem in retrospect that by trying to settle not only an old score, but an ongoing one with my husband (that is, why does he always get to have the career?) I was putting my energy in the wrong place. My anger, and a terrible feeling of being stuck and not moving forward with my life, was the result.

I had to break that unproductive pattern of thinking in order to let go of my rage and get on with my life. Like Sher, I came to the conclusion that the opposite of rage must be patience, whether it applied to developing a new career or connections to my new community.

So What Can You Do About All This Anger?

As the title of this chapter suggests, my advice is to clearly get past it, and the quicker the better. To me, the real threat of anger is that if it goes unchecked, it can turn into bitterness, a label I would run a mile to avoid having pinned on me. Just the idea that I may sound bitter in these pages upsets me because I truly have nothing to feel bitter about and am grateful I have been able to move on with my new life at home.

Anger, I believe, is fine but only up to a certain point. It's usually a short term condition. But to be bitter? That's a life sentence I never want. We have had a life experience which most people, despite their silence on the subject, would absolutely love to have had and that is something that simply must never be forgotten.

During my early days of re-entry, when my professional dreams just wouldn't gel, I was asked constantly that given the hassles I was facing upon return, would I have changed things? Would I have rather stayed home in Canada and never moved around? Never. Despite the anger and resentment that I have had to shed in the years since our return, I can honestly say that I wouldn't exchange my expat memories and experience for a perfectly renovated house or top level job. All right, maybe the renovated house would be nice!

Getting Past It

I had a very good reason for putting all the possible reasons for anger front and center in this chapter before focusing on strategies to combat the feelings. Not only is it good to get it all out, it is important to *validate* your anger. I have found when working with re-entering people, young and old, that before they can move on, they need to stand still for a minute and have a good scream. So go ahead, scream in agreement over any of the issues I have mentioned that make you angry. Add a few to the list if you want. It's OK to be mad.

And then, as I tell my teenage daughter when she is consumed by adolescent angst, get over it! As a beginning, as my swami would tell me, learn to turn your negative thoughts into positive ones.

Geraldine Bown, whom I met at the Working Internationally Now conference in Milan I told you about earlier, is a powerful and inspiring British speaker and workplace consultant. "Anger is an emotion that is full of energy," she advises. "Take that energy and channel it into something else, something productive."

Work Expectations Falling Flat Isn't Always Bad

Like so many expat wives who have been deprived of visas, other working papers, and a structured work life abroad, when I came back to Canada, I dreamed about working full time. I didn't really think beyond the paycheque. If I had, I would have realised I couldn't sit all day in one place and punch a clock. Think long and hard before plunging into that situation. Do you really want to be in an office eight hours or more a day if you are lucky enough to have a choice? Do you want to become a cubicle person? If the job is so fantastic, perhaps your answer is a resounding yes. But for a mediocre job that may cost you more than it pays in child care expenses, extra cars, new clothes, and so on?

After everything else professional in my life seemed to constantly hit brick walls, people who know me well and heard I was looking for full time employment, asked me point blank if I had lost my mind. They seemed to know better than I did that I would be like a caged animal in an office. More critical, there was no way my household could survive with me in the full time labour force. That is, survive the way it has for the entire life of my marriage.

We all return from abroad as different people with new skills and experience. Living abroad shakes us up and makes us re-evaluate who we are and what we want from life. While we may feel angry in the short term that no one seems to want to take advantage of all that experience (a common lament) it is still something that can never be taken away from us. The right person may come along one day who wants to capitalise on our way of seeing things. If that sounds remarkably similar to the search for a perfect marriage partner, it's because in many ways the situations are the same, right down to the same frustrations we felt when trying to date (the old, what's wrong with me? kicks in). I hate to use this word yet again, patience, but if I could learn it, I believe anyone can. Your professional expectations may need to be reshaped (not lowered) in order to avoid getting angry. A work situation which sounds so positive (probably because you can't have it), may in fact turn your life upside down.

Releasing Some of the Financial Pressure That Causes Anger

This is a tricky issue to address because it depends on personal choice. The question you may want to ask is this: How much money does your family *need* as opposed to *want?* The new age simplicity movement, (much of which I personally agree with) means scaling down our lives of the kind of unnecessary stuff that puts a burden on both home and the planets resources. This new way of thinking places a lot of emphasis on people understanding the distinction between need and want.

Overseas, we all engage in belligerent spending, especially those of us who were posted to countries where consumer goods (like books or toys for our kids) couldn't be found. We travel offshore, load up a suitcase, and throw whatever we want into it with the fighting mantra: I deserve it! This may have indeed been the case if you were living in a hardship setting. Those belligerent purchases represented rewards.

You are home now, however, living in cities that are presumably easier to get around in and certainly with no shortage of giant super stores of all descriptions to buy the things you need. You are also back in the land of advertising and hype which tells you how much you are supposed to want in order to fit in. Do you need any of that stuff being hawked in magazines or speciality shopping channels on television? I don't think so. Do you want it? It's OK to admit you do. Sometimes anger erupts when you want something and there simply is no money in your budget (now that you are home) to buy it nor any of the excuses which worked overseas (like unavailability).

When the subjects of work, financial pressures, guilt, and hype all come together to confuse you and make your head spin, ultimately you have to make a choice. Are you willing to live on less if it means retaining flexibility in your work hours (to be available to your children) or to be able to stop banging your head against the wall trying to get hired by people who think you are an alien? If you aren't willing to downscale your life (and let's face it, after the unreal fairy tale world of some expatriates with servants it can be really difficult to revert back to ordinary life) then it will become necessary to find work that pays at whatever cost.

I'm the kind of person who has been trying for years to do with less which believe me, runs completely contrary to my very spoiled upbringing (My mother died suddenly when I was twelve, leaving me with a grief-stricken yet doting father who equated money with love. It took me years to convince him that love was a more direct route to my heart than his check book). It also took me two long years after moving home to a very materialistic North American city to allow my natural principles on this issue to firmly take hold again. I should qualify my comments though. When I say I am willing to live on less I have told my husband that proper beauty salon hair colour (I make too much of a mess doing it myself) four times a year is a non-negotiable item and also finally convinced him of the necessity of a cleaning lady. Once my partner figured out I was serious about essentially doing more (writing, nurturing, and volunteering are my own chosen professions) but earning less, we sat down together and figured out how we would do it without throwing a hissy fit every time we discussed some item we may want but certainly don't need.

Quieting Down on the Home Front

For those who were lucky enough to have had inexpensive household help on posting, laundry now left on the floor to rot quickly becomes an issue when it is you who has to pick it up, wash it, and maybe iron it too. There is usually a honeymoon homemaker period when the ability to do things by yourself, without being watched all the time, comes as a relief. This lasts about a week.

So when one of the partners and the children too are still behaving as if little elves clean up when they are sleeping, it's time to take action or risk becoming a very angry mother martyr. I have since eased up on my family a bit, but when I first realised that I was going to be Molly Maid just because I was the one at home looking for work, I quickly put that idea to bed and the entire family to work. Sunday mornings we became the clean team and cut a swath through our house with rags, vacuum, and window cleaners flying. Of course everyone began to dread getting up on Sunday morning and I quickly amended the routine and finally hired someone to help me. But I made my point: we all live in the house so we can all take care of it. In the process, my kids became darn good house cleaners. I don't make my teenage daughter clean toilets any more but she certainly knows how, and both her and her brother automatically offer assistance when they see me cleaning or doing anything related to the house. Out of my anger grew self-sufficient children and a family who made thankless work worth less so simply by saying, "Thank you Mom." How's that for a positive spin on housecleaning?

Rules of the Road for Your Warrior

Three words helped calm me down about the amount of travel my partner has to do: *quid pro quo*. Translate the Latin in which ever way you wish, but I translate it as Super Elite Air Miles or the reward program of whatever airline your road warrior is keeping in the air. Far from being upset now when he has to travel, my first words are, "Which airline?" I have first claim on his air miles and I have used them for all sorts of family and professional purposes. Moreover, I feel I earned them because as he now admits, without me at home, he couldn't take off as easily as he can.

I am also thoroughly convinced that e-mail was invented solely for road warriors to communicate with their partners. It's perfect. There is no tone in e-mail so you can dash off a quick witty note instead of getting down and dirty and depressed. It's also a great way to keep your children in touch with their father.

Ironically, the worst part of road warrior travel can be when the warrior comes home. You usually manage to hold things together while he's away, but the minute he walks in the door, you are ready with a list of things he has to do. (My husband told me this phenomenon is known in road warrior circles as the *honeydo syndrome,* as in, "Honey, do this, Honey, do that. . .") Naturally, your partner gets upset (he's exhausted after all from working long hours on the road, something we push out of our minds) and you both circle each other like animals in a dance of anger that hasn't any chance of leading to a mating dance no matter how much the returning warrior may wish that to be the case.

You must learn to establish time for reconnection upon his return. It can be a coffee in the morning, a dinner date, or a weekend away. We took up golf again and found it a very neutral way to be together after one of his long journeys. Walking a beautiful fairway and engaging in such intense conversation as 'did you see where my ball went?' provides safe and relaxing exercise. If not on the links, try to set aside time for the two of you to remember why you got married in the first place. A nice quiet dinner out works well too. But don't ruin it by feeling guilty that you are spending time away from your kids. Give yourself a break here.

Helping Friends and Family Understand

Now that you understand your partner, how do you make friends and family understand? Just for a minute, stop and turn around that statement. Do you understand your friends and family? Let's be honest about the level of self absorption we fall into when we come home. Part of that comes from everybody literally taking our temperature every few minutes (happy to be home? happy now? happier?) as we dissect and analyse our new lives from every conceivable angle. I am not suggesting that you stop talking altogether about your previous life, but once in a while, step back and honestly try to analyse just how often you might speak of life abroad without asking about life at home.

Friendships and family relationships work best when they are played out on two way streets and not just one way from us to them. If you want people to respect your experiences then the reverse must also apply. Of course this can sometimes be difficult when you do ask questions and get monosyllabic responses.

It's like when you were living abroad and writing everyone regularly and getting no responses except 'nothing worth writing about happens around here'. How many times have you heard that excuse? But you must persist if you are going to re-establish connections with old friends and make new ones too. Yes, your life abroad was interesting but believe it or not, people do interesting things at home too. Ask them.

Sort Through the Muddle

For those of us who return home for good at mid-life, it is easy to confuse what may be both the physical changes (ageing) with re-entry fatigue. And those existential dilemmas (what do I do now?) face everyone to some degree at any point in their life. Sit down and make a list of challenges now confronting you, certainly the ones making you feel angry, and compare them to the challenges that anyone would feel regardless of moving around. See how many overlap and then try to address them separately.

Wake Up and Enjoy Being Home

Making a full recovery from the repatriation experience is like waking up after having a good night's sleep. You feel optimistic about the day ahead. You begin to feel more like your own self, a person who can and will get involved and feel better about life. That old adage that if you smile at a person, they will smile back definitely holds true. Believe me. Once I wasn't walking around looking miserable and hard done by, my new world did indeed smile back at me. You do, finally, confidently, believe that the best is truly yet to come.

Welcome home!

SELF-ESTEEM AND A NEW ENVIRONMENT

BY DR. KIRSTEN THOGERSEN

*"Sense of self arises not only through discourse with others
but is our discourse with others."*

– Dr. Kenneth Gergen

Twenty years ago, conventional wisdom among psychologists was that selfhood, that is, each person's inner reality or emotional state of mind, was fixed, formed like an unchanging soul substance during the first three years of life. My profession has since learned this is not the true story about self-esteem and identity.

In modern psychology, we now speak about a constructed self, an identity which extends outwards and incorporates the social life around us. This updated version of self-esteem and identity throws new light on the psychological environment of expatriates and repatriates. We now know, for instance, that moving around and settling down in different cultures seriously impacts on our self-esteem and the way we perceive ourselves.

If self-esteem and identity are influenced to a greater extent by our environment, then the significance of where we live as it relates to our mental health becomes critical. We are certainly more capable now than in the past of understanding at least one reason why it is so difficult to move: We are forced to reinvent our self and re-build our self-esteem every time we change our cultural environment.

An individual's interpretation of his or her social world plays a key role in helping that person construct and maintain a self-image. The surrounding culture can nourish our identity. Consequently, if we have no means of expressing, exchanging, or being recognised by the culture in which we operate (even for a short period of time while we adjust), we are in great danger of suffering from a very fragile self-esteem. The more naïve we are about our environment, the more fragile our self-esteem.

A well-orchestrated sense of identity and understanding of self is crucial for mental health anywhere. The stronger the feeling of our true self, the higher the degree of mental health this person can attain. When we have lived for a period of at least two years in the same place most of us will be well contained in our personal habits and routines with a balanced rhythm for each and every day. The culture, the way we organise our day, right down to the very house we call home, all play a profound role in framing our identity. Together, these things form an alliance, building our security and sense of self.

Often we live utterly unaware of this alliance and its significance until it is lost. Loss of identity can open the floodgates to a wide spectrum of psychological difficulties. Depression, fatigue, eating disorders, anxiety and phobias are just a few of the most common psychological reactions stemming from the sense of deprived identity. That is why, for the most part, psychotherapy focuses on assisting individuals to grasp the essential life skill of being able to feel who they are.

Mobility and Self-Esteem

Moving and settling down in a new culture is a dangerous threat to our sense of individual identity. Right after an international move there is a never-ending stream of changes wherever we look. These changes extend inside ourselves. We cannot see through the social world easily as before. Social laws and rules can't be interpreted the same way. What we think we understand often only counts for part of the truth. Events cannot be foreseen easily. Unpredictability and change has suddenly become an every day reality and life condition rather than an exception.

It is human instinct in its simplest form to compare ourselves with those around us. We recognise, we judge, and we form opinions. In short, it is a principal cornerstone in self-identification to measure ourselves in comparison with our surroundings. We form opinions, somewhat automatically, not always consciously. Through a casual glance, we customarily distinguish who and what people are – their social status, economic standing, and to a limited extent even their ideologies. When we see couples chatting in the park, we empathise and form ideas of what they are talking about. Such daily interpretations of social content play a dramatic role in influencing and structuring our sentiments for who we are both as people and as individuals.

But when we move to another culture, we cannot do that. Our cultural know-how is minimised. What psychologists call 'meaning-making' is significantly constrained for a period, until we have integrated into the new culture. Therefore, our sense of self and self-confidence is low for a while. It has to be that way since self-confidence is directly proportional to cultural know-how.

Self-Esteem and Re-entry

When we re-enter our own culture, the risk factors to our self-esteem and identity become even more complex. For, on top of the move and the change of culture as already described, at home we become confused in what I would like to refer to as 'cultural purpose.' We realise that we do not see what we thought we saw and worst of all, we (our selves) have changed. Moving out turned out to be a one-way ticket.

There is no such thing as going home. There is only an illusion – a mirage in the desert. We think we see water but the moment we reach out for it, it turns out to be just a reflection of light. We believe we are going home, but 'home' has turned out to be just a reflection of memory and nostalgia.

Unless people at home have moved and lived internationally themselves, they do not understand much of where you are coming from. The difference between the home culture and the international culture is huge. You have changed. The speed at which you operate will likely be higher than for those around you and you are used to a higher level of stimulation. Often, you will feel as though people at home are thinking very slowly. They are not, in fact, they are just thinking at a pace which is consistent with the demands of their culture.

There is no way you will ever again be assimilated with a group of people who have not been travelling like yourself. You, of course, will start to change and learn new things from the moment you put your feet down on your homeland. However, things will never be the same as before in terms of belonging to a home country. You are all alone, at sea.

In my work as a clinical psychologist, I have found that realising this 'destiny of loneliness' is the turning point for many repatriates. This is the point when they really begin to get new ideas of how to go on with their lives. This where they realise that they have to in a way, 'split themselves up,' only showing small parts and keeping 'secrets.' In order to grow, however, repatriates have to find a way to contain their past without hurting themselves trying to constantly integrate what cannot be integrated.

Moving around and settling down in new cultures changes people profoundly. It's true we are very flexible and we can re-create our selves. But we should be aware of the limitations on our flexibility: it will take several years before we once again find our cultural purpose and know-how at home, and those years will be marked by low self-esteem.

Moreover, we cannot change things back to the way they were before. That is a good thing, though. At least it is supposed to be so.

Dr. Kirsten Thogersen is a clinical psychologist currently living in Beijing. She has 15 years of experience working in international communities.

BIBLIOGRAPHY AND OTHER RESOURCES

BOOKS

Expatriate

Pascoe, Robin (1992). *Culture Shock! A Wife's Guide*. Singapore: Times Editions. ISBN 1-85733-196-6

——— (1993) *Culture Shock! A Parent's Guide*. Singapore:Times Editions. ISBN 1-55868-425-5

Storti, Craig (1991). *The Art of Coming Home*. Yarmouth, ME: Intercultural Press. ISBN 1-877864-47-1

Pollock, David C. and Van Reken, Ruth E. (1999) *The Third Culture Kid Experience, Growing Up Among Worlds*. Yarmouth, ME: Intercultural Press. ISBN 1-877864-72-2

Career and Transition

Parfitt, Joanna (1998). *A Career in Your Suitcase*. Summertime Publishing. ISBN 0-9529453-0-4

Bridges, William (1980). *Transitions, Making Sense of Life's Changes*. New York: Addison-Wesley Publishing. ISBN 0-201-00082-2

——— (1995). *JobShift*. New York: Perseus Publishing. ISBN 0-201-48933-3

Kirk, Janis Foord (1996). SurvivAbility: Career Strategies for the New World of Work. Kirkfoord Communications Inc. ISBN 0-969593-61-9

Sher, Barbara (1979). *Wishcraft, How To Get What You Really Want*. New York: Ballantine Books ISBN 0-345-34089-2

Sher, Barbara (1994). *I Could Do Anything, If I Only Knew What it Was*. New York: Dell. ISBN 0-440-50500-3

Yate, Martin (1987) *Knock 'Em Dead, The Ultimate Job Seeker's Handbook.* Adams Publishing. ISBN 1-55850-433-8

Inspiration, Health, Relationships

Breathnach, Sarah Ban (1995). *Simple Abundance, A Daybook of Comfort and Joy.* New York: Warner Books. ISBN 0-446-51913-8

Lerner, Dr. Harriet (1997) *The Dance of Anger, A Woman's Guide to Changing Patterns of Intimate Relationships.* New York: Harper Collins. ISBN 0-06-091565-x

Sheehy, Gail (1998). *The Silent Passage.* New York: Pocket Books. ISBN 0-671-56777-2

———— (1996) *New Passages: Mapping Your Life Across Time.* New York: Ballantine Books. ISBN 0-345-40445-9

Please note that all of these books are available at www.amazon.com

ORGANISATIONS, CONTACTS AND WEB SITES

Expatriate

The Expat Expert · *www.expatexpert.com*

This is my own web site for families of the international work force. Lots of excerpts from books, opinion and links to other sites.

Outpost Expatriate Information Center · *www.outpostexpat.nl*

This is the mega-site of Outpost, the family services center established by Royal Dutch/Shell and available free to anyone with an internet connection.

Expat Exchange · *www.expatexchange.com*

An on line expatriate community with lots of info and links for expats and repats. One of the first expat communities to go on line.

Escape Artist · *www.escapeartist.com*

A super expat site filled with tons of information and an on line magazine.

Global Nomads · *globalnomads.association.com*

A site about third culture kids and all the issues related to raising children on the move.

Globalnetwork · *www.globalnetwork.co.uk*

A site that is part of the Daily Telegraph newspaper – within its Expat Living section you will find archived articles, information, specialists and hundreds of links to other expatriate web sites.

Words That Work · website.lineone.net/~wordsthatwork

The Expat Experts providing useful books and links to organisations and resources about expatriate life.

Expatmoms · *www.geocities.com/expatmoms*

A site created by a repatriated expat mom for other expatriate mothers everywhere.

Career Web Sites

Career City Women's Center · *www.careercity.com*

Monsterboard · *www.monsterboard.com*

e-Lance · *www.e-lance.com*

Monster Talent Market · *www.talentmarket.monster.com*

Free Agent · *www.freeagent.com*

Guru · *www.guru.com*

eWork Exchange · *ework.com*

Please note that off any of these listed URLS you can find links to even more web sites which may prove valuable to you.

INDEX